3rd Edition

I'TS A GOOD DAY
TO BE A REBEL

HOW TO TURN YOUR PASSION INTO A BUSINESS, SELF-FUND IT, BUILD A KICKASS BRAND & LIVE A DELICIOUSLY FEARLESS LIFE!

ALEXANDRA CARVALHO

Written by Alexandra Carvalho

Cover Design by Danielle Jansenn

Rainbow Hair: Ruth Bocock at Tara Rose Salon
Founded by Tara Rose Kidd

This book is dedicated to that rare breed of people—the misfits, the weirdos, the bold, the crazy, and the extravagantly rebellious. The ones who are geeky, goofy, oddly fascinating, and passionately driven, who never quite fit in…

The ones who refuse to conform, who want to choose to stand outside the lines, find their own unique power and self-expression.

For those who feel that wild, unstoppable fire in their belly, daring to start their own venture.

For those who understand that in today's world, the Social and Digital Media landscape is a playground of endless possibilities.

I see you. This book is for you, written with the wish that I had something like this when I took my leap—terrified yet wildly excited!

Here's your Rebel guide to living a fearless, unapologetic life!

To my mum & my nana who raised me with so much love and ever since I was little telling me to always look for what makes me happy and giving me room to make my choices and support me no matter how crazy it got.

To my Nana for being so theatrical and able to transform the most mundane things into beautiful cinematic experiences. For letting me watch her, as a little girl, draw her eyebrows with turquoise eyeliner, and for putting me on stage when I was six, telling me I was a star!

To my mum, for saving herself from a monster and becoming my hero by saving me. For giving me a life filled with love, and for showing me what it means to be the strongest person I know.

Dear Rebel Readers,

I can hardly believe we're here on the third edition, of *"It's a Good Day to Be a Rebel"* and the last and final one for this book series. These new chapters were deeply personal, and this is the first time I'm sharing these stories with you rebels and it just beautifully aligns with a new chapter in my life, so it feels really fitting to end the season of *"It's a Good Day to Be a Rebel"* with this last 3rd edition! *And leave room for more magic of a new book in the future!*

Thank you for making the previous edition reach 4th & 7th on Amazon.com, under Social Media, when I started I didn't even think anyone would want to read my book!

So much has happened since the last time I wrote to you. Yes, this is like my diary of a rebel to you. *(That's a good podcast idea, isn't it? I really need to work on that!)*

One of the first new things you might notice with this edition is my name. Have you noticed it's not Alexandra Maia anymore? It's Alexandra Carvalho. In the past three years, I took a big, bold step in my emotional healing journey by removing my father's surname. It still feels strange…After all it's been a part of me for 39/40 years. When you remove a family name that's been with you since birth, you realize how long it takes to adjust. This was a significant part of my healing—to let go of a name that carried rejection and pain. I thought to myself… Why am I carrying around a name that's been synonymous with pain, rejection, left me believing for years that all I deserved from men were breadcrumbs….What?! This is crazy I realized…! When people get divorced, they often remove their spouse's name. Well, I divorced my father. Or rather, he divorced me by never truly wanting me. So it was time to remove a part of me that didn't' belong or made sense to me

So, that's one of the first changes you'll notice in this third edition.

I'm very proud to have done it. Yes, it still feels odd, like a part of me is missing, but maybe it should be missing. I wanted to honor my mom and grandma, who raised me and saved me. If not for their incredible love, everything with my father could have caused so much more pain. They infused me with strength, and I'm grateful to carry the name Carvalho forward!

As I sat down to share everything new, these chapters felt very vulnerable. I'm opening up about things I never shared in the past 3 years...About my new business venture, the challenges of raising capital, and going through some dark shaky times.

How do you find your way back? How do you come back from feeling like you're going to lose it all, especially when so much is out of your control?

Despite the bumpy ride, some of the coolest, most incredible things happened to Alex's House of Social, becoming catalysts for new opportunities. Like the re-launch of my exclusive consultancy Rebel Club after it had failed previously!

The Free Rebel Academy at the time of writing this book is now streaming 74 free classes gained a whole new revamp your student dashboard now looks just like the Netflix interface! It really should be called Netflix but I don't want to get into problems with Netflix!

But the stories on these new chapters pull the curtain back on what happened behind the scenes in these past 3 years, that might have been some of the most challenging in 9 years in business. At the time I couldn't really share in full all that was happening but now I can, and we can continue where we left of...!

I'm honored to share them with you, hoping they inspire and remind you that life is far from perfect...But that if we don't jump forward and go after new experiences, and that every decision we make needs to be to get us closer to our goals and dreams...What are we doing with this extraordinary opportunity of being alive!

Dear rebels, we are here to be bold, to color outside the lines, to not conform. We are here to believe in our ideas and bring them to life. It's your vision that matters—not what others think or say. Remember, it won't be their name on your grave. It'll be yours.

In the past couple of years, I've lost very special people. It's a sad reminder of how precious life is and why we must hold on to it *now.* So, if you have that idea, that project, stop the excuses and overthinking. Just try. Because when you try, you are already winning. In a world where most don't even attempt, where so many judge and criticize without taking action themselves, your courage to try is already a victory!

I want you to win. I want you to find happiness, and never stop exploring what brings you joy. On my last chapter of this book I open up about some of my new realizations arounf happiness and what new venture that means for me….

I hope you see this book as a manual. Pick it up at any chapter, or read it from start to finish. Highlight sections, add sticky notes, make it your own. There's a lot of practical advice here for you to use, keep it by your side on your desk or your bag. Lend it to a friend who needs that courage, that as needs some rebellious juice in their life!

I hope it's the guide you need to live your most delicious rebellious life!

Happy reading, your Rebel, Alex

3RD EDITION GUEST REBELS

Breaking Free From Abuse: The Courage to Rebel and Rise Again By Fernanda Carvalho

I'm really humbled to have my mum share a little big snippet of her life with you. How she saved herself from an abusive husband and, in return, became my hero by giving me a life full of love and showing me that even when you lose it all and go through a war, you can rebuild your life as a divorced single woman, venture into a male-dominated industry, and work your way up. For many of you who follow my content, or who will read the first chapter of this book, you will understand why she is my hero. But this time, I really wanted it to come from her.

For many women who might be in abusive relationships, considering staying for the sake of your kids, or thinking you can't raise your children as a single divorced mother—this chapter is for you.

Thank you, Mum, for sharing with us a vulnerable yet powerful part of your story.
You're my world!

The Power of Pacing Your Peaks
by Helen Farmer

The way I met Helen (I'm not sure if she remembers… hehe) was quite serendipitous. I was sitting in a coffee shop during my first year of House of Social, circa 2016/17. I happened to be seated very close to her (I didn't know who she was at the time) and couldn't help but overhear her conversation with a friend. They were discussing social media—something about Facebook or Instagram. She was so passionate, and I just remember really wanting to jump in and help with whatever she was trying to figure out. After a while of biting my lips, I leaned in and interrupted them (hoping they wouldn't think I was a stalker!)—and I can't even remember what I said! From that moment on, I started following her journey and watched her continuous growth with her community, from Facebook to Instagram, to radio, and now her latest adventure: a children's book!

What I love about Helen, apart from her authentic spirit, are the challenges she sets for herself and how she keeps reinventing and creating more adventures for her! For Helen, age is never an obstacle to start something new that she loves! I knew Helen's story could inspire many of you. I wasn't sure if she was going to say yes to me… and guess what? *She did!* So, I can't wait for you to read her chapter!

CONTENTS:

1. Finding Your Power Despite Adversity   13
2. How to Find Your Way When You're Lost   35
3. *The Perfect Day to Leap*   45
   Bootstrapping Guide
4. *Stuff They Don't Teach You at School*   61
   Entrepreneurship Toolkit
5. *Social Media Winning Creative Strategies*   67
   My Blueprint
6. How to Build a Kickass Brand   85
7. Swimming with Sharks with Kindness   101
8. To Stand Out You Can't Be Trying to Fit In   107
9. *Going into Unchartered waters*   113
   Raising Capital & Trademarking NEW
10. When to Walk Away *NEW*   127
11. The Come Back Kid *NEW*   133
12. The Pursuit of Happiness *NEW*   143
13. Rebel Academy & Rebel Club   147
14. Guest Chapters – *NEW*   153
15. Breaking Free From Abuse: The Courage to   154
    Rebel and Rise Again By Fernanda Carvalho
16. The Power of Pacing Your Peaks   159
    by Helen Farmer
17. Client Case studies   163
18. 20 Steps to Turn Your Passion into   173
    Profitable Mini Empire

I'TS A GOOD DAY
TO BE A REBEL

CHAPTER 1

Finding Your Power Despite Adversity

I wrote this chapter for anyone who has faced or is currently facing bullying, had an absent parental figure while growing up, or dealt with any kind of adversity. I'm sharing some of my own personal stories that I haven't shared so openly before. I'm sharing in the hope that you won't feel so alone, that whatever you may be going through, you won't let it define your future or who you become. Our traumas are real, and we need to confront them, put in the work, and become the best versions of ourselves.

If you're going through a tough time or have been in the past, I want you to know there is a way to take all that adversity and turn it to your advantage. Your past does not define your present or future. When I started this wild journey called entrepreneurship and decided to go 100% self-funded, I didn't realize how much of what sets you up for success can be drawn from what you went through when you were younger. When you piece it all together later in life, many past events start to make sense as to why you're doing what you're doing now.

A lot of the adversity and bullying I experienced during my childhood and my 20s has turned into my advantage because adversity builds resilience. So, if you're reading this and you have faced adversity, know that this can unlock so much strength for you. It prepares you for all the challenges yet to come! And drum roll… The best news? You'll likely bounce back way quicker than someone who has never faced much adversity. It's just reality. When you've dealt with bullying or any kind of hardship, you build 'muscle,' a thicker skin to handle tough situations. For me, it became part of the fabric of my entrepreneurship journey.

Choosing to go on this journey of self-discovery, figuring out what makes you happy, setting yourself free (a.k.a. letting go of what's holding you down), and taking that leap is going to be the most exhilarating ride of your life!

So, where are you now? You might be in one or more of these scenarios:

- Going 'all in' on starting your own business.
- Quitting that toxic 9-5 job and looking for another job with better career opportunities.
- Realizing you want to completely change careers.
- Taking a break and going traveling for a while to rediscover yourself.
- Getting a 9-5 just to cover your basic financial needs while dedicating all your free time to your side hustle.
- Leaving behind toxic, negative friends and environments.
- Moving to a new country.
- Still loving and respecting your family but wanting to live your own life, not what they want for you.

PORK & CHEESE

My mum and Nana moved from Portugal to the UK, Guildford in Surrey to be precise, in 1994 when I was nine, turning ten. Let me paint you a quick picture: I would walk to school or take the bus in Lisbon's bright, sunny, picturesque city. I wore jeans and t-shirts, had super long blonde hair, and most of my time at school was spent hanging out at the coffee shop — I was never a good student! As a kid in Lisbon, in the early 1990s, my mum would often tell me I was so much like how I am today. I was always making noise, talking, talking, even to myself. She would sometimes say, "I'll give you fifteen euros if you stay quiet for one hour!" I definitely used this to my advantage! Haha… One of my favorite memories was when I figured out I could make my own stickers instead of buying them. I loved this wrapping paper but wanted stickers from the illustrations, so I used transparent sticky paper (the kind we used to protect schoolbooks) to make stickers. But I wasn't satisfied. I put them in a little tin and went downstairs, onto the street, to sell them. Or at least, I tried to! I vividly remember how much I loved being out there, trying to sell those stickers, and volunteering to sell the church's Christmas calendar. I'd stand outside the church hustling it!

Then, in 1994, I found myself in a uniform shop in Guildford, wearing a thick grey and maroon uniform with layers up to my ears! WTF had just happened?! And why was it grey outside every single day?!I was nine and didn't speak English. I could barely understand it. Sure, I had listened to a lot of Frank Sinatra and watched 1950s movies in English. On my first day of school, I was frozen in the cold, feeling like I was in some alternate movie, sitting in the car, heading… well, I didn't even know where. We reached the school gate; my mum held my hand. I was scared. I could feel she was a little nervous, too, trying to be strong for me because, from the gates, we could see this massive school (the typical kind you see in the UK). I'd never seen anything like it before. I'm a city girl. What are these gigantic schools with three football fields? Just the sheer size of it was intimidating. The kids were all in their groups, tight-knit and exclusive, as if you had to be or look a certain way to fit in. Moving to a new country is never easy. Even when I moved from Singapore back to Dubai, it was a little tricky. But when you're nine, it's extra scary!

The next few years were tough. I remember crying every night and asking my mum, "Why?" She kept telling me, "I know you can't see it now, but one day, this is going to make you so strong." And she was right. I didn't understand it at the time, but I trusted her. For two years, I had no friends. I was called "Pork and Cheese" because I was Portuguese. Aren't kids just so creative...? I was laughed at when I had to read out loud in class. When I wasn't in class, school was unbearable because everyone had their groups, from the geeks to the popular ones. Oh yeah, there was definitely a hierarchy! I didn't know what to do with myself during breaks. At lunchtime, I'd get my tray but find no place to sit. I'd either eat alone or, many times, shove the sandwiches into my blazer pockets, head to the

15

bathroom, lock the door, and sit there.

Have you ever been bullied? Or maybe you know someone who has? The saddest part is that bullies are everywhere — at school, in the workplace, even at home, often hiding behind charming personalities. I've faced bullies even in my professional life; clients in the past who turned out to be straight-up bullies.

If you're being bullied or know someone who is, please remember:

- Become self-aware and acknowledge what's happening. Be present and recognize that this is NOT OK.
- Reach out for help. Talk to someone you trust, and speak to more than one person if possible. Sometimes, the first person you reach out to might not be the right one, so don't give up. Call a support line, lean on friends, and avoid being alone for long periods.
- There is no excuse for abuse. It's never acceptable, even if it comes from a friend, colleague, parental figure, or your boss.
- Bullies are great at gaslighting and making you feel it's your fault. Remember, your feelings are real, valid, and should not be ignored.
- You don't have to stay in this situation. Whatever is on the 'other side' will be better than what you're enduring now.

On the way home, after the bus dropped me off, there were neighborhood kids who would taunt me, saying, "You don't belong here," or "Go back home, Pork and Cheese!" I often wondered, are kids naturally like this, or is it just a reflection of what goes on at home, influenced by their parents? One day, they warned me, "If you walk past here tomorrow, we're going to wait for you!" The next day, two kids, a brother and sister, walked with me as we went through an alleyway that led to our estate. And there they were… hiding. Groups on both sides, behind bushes, holding stones and bricks they had taken from a nearby construction site. I'll never forget how I stood still, staring at them. The brother and sister stepped back. I kept looking forward and started walking, head held high, just like my mum always taught me. I remember a huge brick flying inches from my face. It didn't hit me, but I'll never forget its burnt orange color.

One afternoon, my mum went over to confront them, and I think she scared the life out of them!

During this time, I learned how to hang out with the best company ever: me, myself, and I! Going to the shops on the high street was something kids did in groups after school or on weekends. Since I wasn't part of a group, I learned to enjoy doing those things alone. And let me tell you, a lot of people struggle with being on their own.

Do you enjoy your own company?

It's so important to learn to love spending time with yourself. Enjoy your thoughts, be present, and recharge your energy.

When was the last time you did something purely for yourself? Maybe a short solo trip, a visit to the movies, a walk in the park, or a day at the museum or theater? If you haven't, try making it a routine — just as you schedule time for others, schedule time for YOU! And most importantly…

Are you checking in with yourself daily, mentally, physically, and emotionally?

I call it an **Emotional Self-Check-In**. I started this little habit three years ago, and it's made a world of difference.

Every morning, whether I'm making coffee or stretching, I take a moment to pause, breathe, and ask myself:

- How am I feeling today?
- What emotions am I experiencing — happy, worried, anxious, excited?
- If I notice any troubling emotions, I ask, "What is making me feel this way?"

- Then I remind myself of the things I'm grateful for. That usually softens any sadness or stress.
- If needed, I think back to tougher times I've overcome, and that makes current worries seem less daunting.
- Understanding how I feel early in the day helps me set up for whatever lies ahead. If I'm feeling more tired, I remind myself to be extra patient, especially if I have clients.

This whole process takes less than 5 minutes, and the more you do it, the more natural it becomes.

Don't live life on autopilot! You are not a machine. You are made of emotions, physical needs, and mental and holistic elements.

Remember: The more you run on autopilot, the further you drift from your true self and your needs. Unlocking your unique, epic self becomes harder if you do not take the time to be present.

I don't remember when exactly, but there was a day I decided, "I can't beat them, so I'll join them!" And right there, my mission began. I was determined! Every day after school, I learned to speak perfect British English. We lived with Tony (my mum's partner back then), and after school, his son Ben would coach me on mastering that perfect English accent. I wanted to sound just like them, and I did after a while! My fair skin and blonde hair helped me play the part, too.

After two years, I was finally 'accepted' into a group of girls who proudly called themselves the 'geeks.' They were super sweet! Eventually, I moved on to a group of girls who were kind of like the most popular ones. Sounds like one of those teen movies, right?! My mum tells me that teachers used to say it was nearly impossible to keep me quiet. That's consistent with my time back in Lisbon, where my teacher would try everything, moving me around, seating me next to the quietest students, and finally placing my desk right next to hers in a bid to get me to stop talking! When I was sick with appendicitis back in the UK, the teachers mentioned how quiet the classroom was without me.

It was also in the UK that I took my performing arts training to the next level. In Portugal, I had been part of the choir since I was six. On weekends, I attended a performing arts school where I danced, tapped, and sang my heart out. Honestly, I lived for those weekends.

You know when I thought I'd finally made friends? When we graduated and went to prom. We all got ready at my house. You could say we had become good friends! After the prom, we were all so excited because we were headed to Guildford's most popular club, Bojangles! This was the big event we had been looking forward to. I was fifteen. When we got there, we joined the line, and the bouncer started letting people in. But when it was my turn, he asked, "Where's your ID?" "What ID? I don't have one!" I replied. He looked at my friends and said, "You have IDs, don't you?" I saw one of my friends glance back at me as she walked into the club. I said, "They're not letting me in." She looked at me but kept walking. Turns out, they had made fake IDs for each other but left me out. It was 1997, and I didn't have a cell phone, so I crossed the street and called home from a phone box. My mum and Tony came to pick me up.

I know what you're thinking… that's awful… and it was. But at fifteen, this wasn't the first time I had been left out, shut out, or left on the street. More on that later!

Crushing Bullies:

- **Don't Show Fear:** Bullies thrive on fear. They love to see you shrink, so do the opposite. Stand tall, speak up, look them in the eye, and, if needed, just ignore them!
- **Establish Boundaries:** Set both verbal and physical boundaries. Keep your physical distance, and if needed, tell them directly, "I need space," or "That needs to stop." No need to over-explain. Be short, direct, and move on. If they don't change, avoid engaging with them.

A few scripts to help you stand your ground with bullies:

- "I understand you're my boss/mum/colleague, but that doesn't give you the right to talk to me this way. It offends me, and you're crossing my boundaries. I respect you, and I expect the same in return. Until you can treat me with respect, I'm taking some space from this relationship."
- "When you feel you're able to speak to me kindly, you can call, text, or email me."
- "Don't contact me or talk to me until you can treat me with respect."

Adversity Builds Resilience

Adversity is a funny thing. When it shows up, you've got two choices: you either draw strength from it and use it as fuel to rise, or you let it become a roadblock for the rest of your life.

My mum is my hero, and my Nana is right up there too. I've never really shared much detail as to why she is my hero until now. Growing up, her role in my life answered many questions about the choices I've made and the person I've become. I know not everyone can say the same about their mum, just like I can't say the same about my father. My mum and Nana, despite all the struggles — not having much money, my father being destructive — they gave me so much love (and still do, even though Nana has passed). They always said, "No matter what you decide to do, make sure it makes you HAPPY!" Happiness was always the core focus at home. It was the ultimate goal, the ROI.

Choosing happiness over everything is so important. For example, picking a job where you know the culture and managers are supportive beats staying at a company that pays more but makes you miserable.

They empowered me to go out into the world and search for my own happiness. My Nana, back in her early days, was an opera singer diva, and she carried that swagger into her later years. She and her opera friends would let me dress up and perform little shows for them!

If this book can give you even a tiny ounce of that love, if these chapters make you feel more empowered, loved, and supported, then my purpose is fulfilled. Pass this feeling on to others. Let it ripple.

My family is originally from Angola, a former Portuguese colony. In 1975, Angola gained independence, and a civil war erupted. My mum had dreams of becoming a lawyer, just like her father. But when the war broke out, all white Portuguese people were at risk and told to get on planes to leave. My family lost everything. Bank accounts were frozen, the house was shot at, my father's coffee farm and lands were taken over. The dreams they had, the life they knew — it was all lost.

There's so much I could write about the stories my mum and Nana shared about the war in Angola — how my father built a bunker for survival, how they traded items for extra food rations… I've told my mum she should write that book, too! My parents eventually boarded a refugee plane, and on that night, my mum had never felt more nervous. My father had placed diamonds under her tongue so when they landed, they'd have some money. They left with just one suitcase in their hands; everything else was gone.

My father is the person who has hurt me the most in life. But he's also the reason I've learned that we can work on ourselves and not let the actions of parental figures create emotional traumas that mess up our lives forever or stop us from achieving our dreams.

If someone tells you at a young age that you're worthless, you might believe it. But remember, those words come from someone who is broken. You can shed those false beliefs. Say to yourself, "That was said by someone who is broken, and that is not my truth. I am worthy. I am amazing. I am capable. And I can do anything I set my mind to."

You have to create new core beliefs based on real truths about yourself and the person you aspire to be.

21

- Start working on your self-awareness. Recognize patterns that need changing.
- Silence those voices in your head that drag you down.
- Make a list of all the things you're great at.
- Write down the person you want to be — for yourself.
- Think about how you want others to feel around you.
- What type of legacy do you want to leave behind? How do you want to be remembered?
- What fears and old baggage do you want to shed?

If you had parental figures who mistreated you, whether it was blunt or subtle — gaslighting, ignoring you, favoring others — and you can tell it left you with traumas or wrong self-beliefs like "I'm not good enough," I want you to acknowledge that you can break free from these false beliefs. You do not have to carry these wrong beliefs for the rest of your life. They can hold you back from achieving your dreams more than you might realize. So, let's get smart, develop the self-awareness to identify what needs healing, and put in the work to rediscover our true selves.

Yes, it's possible!

I'll continue refining the rest of the text in the same tone. Let me know if there are any sections you'd like me to focus on, or if you'd like me to proceed directly with the following parts.

You are not a prisoner of your past. Those false core beliefs have an expiration date and don't serve your dreams.

By doing the self-work, by choosing to heal, we gain the power to change. We don't have to let the past define who we are today or dictate our future. I see so many people afraid to chase their goals, afraid to take a leap because of the broken, negative things placed in their heads by someone else. If that's you, grab a piece of paper, write down all those hurtful things, and then burn it. Throw it in the trash. Write down a whole list of amazing, new truths about yourself, and plaster them everywhere. Stick them on your phone cover, your fridge, your mirror. Say them to yourself until they become your truth, your new religion!

Finding that mental freedom to let go of the old, false beliefs is the first step. It's not about strategies, tactics, or money.

Once you decide to believe in yourself, everything will start falling into place. You won't fear failure, because you'll know that just trying is a win. This is what will ignite your power from within.

The relationship with my father was abusive, both emotionally and physically. He would smack me really hard at times, for no reason. He rejected me my whole life, and it left me with some unhealthy traumas, especially regarding my relationships with men. His life could be straight out of a jungle adventure story. He grew up in Angola on a coffee farm, spent time in the jungle, fought in the Civil War in the 70s, built a bunker for my mother's family, and eventually got into the diamond business. Sounds fascinating, right? But I've come to understand that my father had some serious traumas that, sadly, turned him into a man who wasn't very kind.

Before and during the war, his behavior began to change, and not for the better. He started drinking heavily, and the physical abuse toward my mum began. When I was born in 1982, he became obsessed. No one could touch or hold me. He kept my mum locked in the house with no access to money, a car, or even basic freedoms. A few times, my mum or neighbors would call the police. They would come, see that my mum was hurt, but my father was such a smooth talker that they'd end up drinking whisky and smoking cigars with him. The aggression continued, as did his obsession with keeping her locked up. One day, my mum says she looked at me as a baby and thought, "This is not the life I want for my child." She knew what she had to do.

One night, she managed to escape. She needed to get a job, find a home, and gather proof of my father's abuse so she could win full custody of me in court and get a divorce. But to do all of this, she couldn't take me with her. She risked losing me because she couldn't provide for me yet. So, she had to leave me behind the night she left. She says she looked at me and whispered, "I won't take long. I'll be right back, and we'll be together forever." She went through extreme measures to gain custody, and I'll just leave it at that. She got a job at DHL sealing envelopes, working every shift she could, weekends included, just so we could have electricity and food on the table. Years later, she became the DHL Country Customer Service Manager for Portugal.

I have so much respect for self-made people. You learn about real hard work. Being in the dirt, putting in the hours, and learning what it takes to get things done. It builds grit and a thick skin that you need for life.

As soon as my father realized what had happened, he ran away with me. For three months, we were in some small town in Portugal. After months of searching, my Nana and a police friend managed to find us, and my father handed me over. According to him, I wasn't myself. Over time, I seemed to become apathetic. I don't remember much of this, or perhaps as a defense mechanism, my brain chose not to. I've since learned that the mind and body can do this in traumatic situations. Here's a passage from Dr. Nicole LePera's book, *How to Do the Work: Recognize Your Patterns, Heal from Your Past, and Create Your Self*:

"Trauma is not just the big things. In fact, it isn't about the size of the trauma at all. It's the impact. It's the way the brain and body receive the impact, and how much support there is to process it."

"If you do not have memories, understand this is a normal, protective human response. Healing does not require us to regain memories, and we don't need to pinpoint the exact reason they don't exist."

A Little Blue Suitcase

My mum had the best relationship with her father, and she truly wanted me to have the same. She tried so hard to make things work with my dad. Instead of immediately cutting him out of my life, she gave him every chance. The years that followed were tough. I spent a few weekends with him, but mostly he just wouldn't show up, and there was no financial support. One time, he got randomly angry at me. He slammed my little blue suitcase shut (I loved that suitcase; I always took it with me, carrying just one sweater inside), opened the apartment door, pushed me outside, and slammed the door. I stood there, staring at that door, determined to get him to open it again. But… I was too short to reach the doorbell. So, I stood on my little suitcase and kept pressing that doorbell for as long as I could.

Nope, didn't work… So, I wandered into the street, found a restaurant, and called home for my mum or Nana to come pick me up. I have other stories, but this one stands out the most. That little blue suitcase was my companion through it all.

You may not even realize you're being emotionally abused, especially when it comes from people close to you — family, partners, work colleagues, or managers. Because we care about them, it's easy to turn a blind eye. But please don't. The more you take this kind of abuse, the more it will drain you, take a toll, and bring you down.

Signs of Mental & Emotional Abuse:

- Name-calling, even if it's framed as a 'joke.'
- Derogatory 'pet names' that make you uncomfortable.
- Yelling, shouting, or using a tone that scares or unsettles you.
- Patronizing comments like, "I know you're trying, but this is beyond what you can understand."
- Embarrassing you in public.
- Making comments about your weight or appearance.
- Belittling your accomplishments.
- Pushing your buttons on purpose.

I remember when I was going through my fitness transformation back in 2015. I lost around 10 kilos, and some colleagues would make 'subtle' jokes about my transformation and my social media posts. At first, I didn't pick up on it. I laughed along, but it kept happening, and I started to feel uncomfortable. That feeling was too familiar, a flashback to the bullying I faced when I first moved to the UK at ten.

Learn to spot these behaviors. Learn to distance yourself from these people, cut them out if you need to, or simply tell them how their actions make you feel. My father called me names, up until the last time we ever spoke — I was probably in my late 20s. When I was younger, he would talk down to me, insult my mum and Nana, and when I'd cry, he'd shout and tell me to be silent. Crying was like having an anxiety attack you couldn't escape from.

My mum always repeated this one piece of advice, over and over, to the point that it has stayed with me forever. Maybe it will help you, too!

She'd say: "Never look down at anyone! Hold your head up and look them right in the eye. Never, ever look down!"

Buddhism helped me forgive my father and find peace. Have I fully gotten over the abandonment or trauma? Not 100%, but it's been 10 years since I've found myself in a self-destructive relationship with men. I realized my relationships mirrored the one I had with my father — after all, he set the blueprint. But as I've said, you can break away from this. This is why I encourage you: look at your patterns.

It's empowering to see that you can change. The first time I told a guy, "No. I don't want to see you anymore because your lack of investment doesn't match what I'm looking for," it was both scary and liberating. I felt like I'd regained power and control.

I've also recently learned that our brains love comfort and patterns. If you believe everything is terrible, guess what? You'll only see the negatives. You're programming your mind to see the worst! If you believe you're not good enough, every challenge will feel harder than it really is. But here's the good news: your mind can be rewired to embrace new, empowering beliefs that help you let go of what's been weighing you down.

You have to release those old chains and reprogram your mindset to work for you, not against you. I'm not an expert in healing traumas; I can only share my journey and what I've learned along the way.

Here are my favorite resources and people who continue to help me in practical ways:

- **The Book:** *How to Do the Work* by Dr. Nicole LePera, The Holistic Psychologist. Check out her Instagram page @theholisticpsychologist. She guides you step-by-step on how to heal from trauma, understand family archetypes, and offers plenty of exercises.
- **Matthew Hussey** teaches you how to communicate better with men, but honestly, a lot of his advice can apply to any relationship — work or personal. He provides scripts and teaches you how to communicate effectively to get your point across. It's amazing how much we struggle with basic communication!
- **The Art of Happiness: A Handbook for Living** by His Holiness, The Dalai Lama.

Questions that have helped me, and might help you too:

- What triggers me?
- What is my emotional and mental response when I'm triggered?
- What's my physical response?
- What am I afraid of?
- What do I need to feel safe?

Betting on Yourself is Always the Right Choice

Remember my sudden move to the UK? When my mum tucked me in at night, she'd say, "One day you'll understand all this…" Many years later, she told me the real reason we left for the UK when I was ten. It was to escape my father and all the destructive abuse.

The following years were just as painful, if not more. I was growing up, longing for a dad who wanted me, but he only pushed me away and rejected me. The rare phone calls we had were filled with hatred and verbal abuse. There was no financial support, even though he was well-off. Later, he returned to Angola and went into the diamond business, where he remains today (I think!).

Since I was little, my biggest dream was to be an actress in New York — a dream that felt so big and far away for a girl from Portugal. I thought I'd spend my whole life hustling to get there. Never in a million years did I imagine I'd make it to New York at twenty!

A theater director gave me a slip of paper with the names of three of the best acting schools in New York and said I needed to get out of Portugal. I left that meeting feeling discouraged. How would we ever afford acting school in New York, let alone get accepted into one? But my mum and Nana always taught me to go after what I loved, no matter what.

So, I sent out my VHS audition tapes to The American Academy of Dramatic Arts (AADA). I didn't even tell my mum or Nana. I didn't think anything would come of it — just a small Portuguese girl, feeling like a tiny fish in the biggest ocean. A couple of months later, in December 2001, I was on a plane to New York for my audition. This was my dream! Tony, a close family friend, took me there. He treated me like a daughter and was so proud that he covered my plane tickets and hotel. We had the most magical time in New York, and I got to see a whole new world.

A few weeks later, I got a letter in the mail saying I'd been accepted. The floor moved beneath my feet! Never, even until today, have I felt a moment that matched this one. For the first time in my life, at nineteen, I felt that "yes" was possible if you just believed that the world is filled with endless possibilities. You just have to reach out and try. I had no idea what would happen next, but that acceptance letter changed everything!

If I hadn't sent that VHS tape, just to try, I never would have lived the most amazing experience of my life.

I bet on myself. I didn't take it too seriously, but I took a chance.

Betting on yourself is always the right choice. No matter the outcome, you will learn, grow, and evolve.

Don't we want that? Yes, we absolutely do! Over the years, working with clients and students, I've seen people be so hard on themselves. How about looking at things with a lighter perspective? Ask yourself: "What's the worst that can happen, really?" and then follow up with, "And is that even the worst?" Because let's be real, things like dying or getting seriously sick — that's the real worst.

My mum is what made it all possible. She said, "I didn't get to live my dream because of the war. Now you have this opportunity at nineteen to go to New York. For the first time, we have money saved. Screw it! We're using it, otherwise what's it for?!" And that's how I made it to New York.

After a year and a half there, the money ran out, and my visa needed renewal. I needed more funds to continue at AADA. I was invited to join their final year program and their Theater Company, but there were no bank loans or extra money left.

There was one person I knew who had money — my father. I took a deep breath, swallowed my pride, found his number, and called to ask for a loan. A loan, not a gift. That call lasted maybe two minutes. It was filled with insults, name-calling, shaming, and him saying I was nothing. He had no idea about my life and had no interest in knowing. It's been like that ever since.

So, life taught me another big lesson: **even when you're living your dream, it can be snatched away.** My New York dream was over. I had to leave the city. What followed was a phase where I felt completely lost, and the world seemed dark. I had tasted and lived my dream — like the TV show *Fame* that I grew up watching: leg warmers, dance classes, singing, acting, learning lines, endlessly walking the streets of New York, sitting on pavements, eating cups of noodles and slices of pizza to save money. Oh boy, did I love that life and my tiny, tiny room!

More on being lost… in the next chapter.

This experience taught me that:

When you bet on yourself, when you take that leap and simply try, **FREAKING AMAZING, EPIC THINGS CAN HAPPEN TO YOU!**

Not because you're relying on luck or someone to make your dreams come true, but because you found the courage to try!

So, young Rebel, especially if you're in your 20s, spread your wings and fly! And honestly, no matter what age you are, please just try. I was 20 when I got to New York, a little girl from a modest background, and there I was. And at that moment, when I saw the NYC skyline, I learned:

EVERYTHING IS POSSIBLE. IT ONLY TAKES COURAGE TO TRY!

LIFE CHANGED FOR ME AT THAT MOMENT IN WAYS I NEVER REALIZED AT THE TIME.

I want you to feel this power inside you. It shifts you from being on the sidelines, dreaming of 'flying,' to actually taking flight. Even if you fall a few times, even if it takes a while to lift off — just this practice will empower you so much!

Yes, there will be nerves; it's normal. But that fire in your belly will burn brighter and propel you to take the leap. Once you take that first step, you'll see that most of the fear was just in your head. And… don't you want to learn, evolve, and challenge yourself? This is your time.

GET KNOCKED DOWN & STILL FLY!

My mum showed me what a warrior looks like — what it means to fight, and how hard work can transform your career. She taught me that you can start with almost nothing and turn it into a gem. We faced hardships in my early years, but she was always strong, solid, and practical. When things went wrong, she'd say, "Okay, let's make a plan and keep moving forward. And always, together, always with your head held high."

She spoiled me with so much love and warmth. There was nothing she wouldn't do for me. After a month of working extra shifts, she bought me a Nintendo Game Boy. She taught me that things don't just fall from the sky; you have to work to earn them. And when you do earn them, your independence and freedom are priceless. That's how you discover your power — when you stand on your own two feet, without relying on anyone else's mercy.

If I was going to venture out and build a business on my own, this is why it became a question of, **Can I do it on my own?**

So please, if you're reading this, be willing to put in the real work. Learn, grow, and taste the satisfaction of your achievements because they will feel infinitely more fulfilling when you've worked for them. They won't be handed to you; they'll be earned.

Learn to build that independence for yourself.

A long time ago, I read a quote from Tony Robbins that stuck with me:

"If you never push yourself to the edge, you'll never see what's on the other side."

Taking a leap can be about anything your heart truly desires — that deep, almost-secret dream you hold within. Maybe it's going back to university, starting that side hustle on weekends, transitioning into a new career, moving to a different country, or finally quitting that 9-to-5 to start your own venture. It could be selling your art, writing a book, or launching your podcast. You'll know it because you'll feel it calling from inside you.

And if you have too many ideas swirling around, unsure which one to start with, just pick one. Any one! There isn't a wrong choice. The quicker you just go for it, the sooner you'll know.

Some Ideas for Your Next Opportunity + Resources:

- **Launch your own merchandise or sell your art** with a POD (print on demand) company – Try Printful, Printify
- **Create your own app** with platforms that have built-in app frameworks - Appypie or Buildfire.
- **Start your own marketplace** - Sharetribe.
- **Build your business or personal brand site** - Wix.
- **Kickstart an e-commerce business** - Shopify or WooCommerce.
- **Leverage your personal brand to coach, consult, or teach.**
- **Sell and create online courses** - Thinkific.
- **Sell your art, set up your own online shop** - Etsy or Pinterest.
- **Create your own NFT project.**
- **Self-publish a book** on Amazon - Amazon KDP.
- **Launch a podcast!** - Try Captivate or Anchor.

Just to list a few, but seriously, you can start almost anything today!

FINDING YOUR POWER

Maybe some of you reading this chapter can relate to these stories. Adversity can make you the strongest version of yourself. Being resilient is like donning a suit of armor, ready for whatever comes your way. You might not get knocked down, but even if you do, you bounce back quicker. We cannot control bad, toxic people. We cannot fix them, and it's not our job to try. If they don't want to change or begin their healing process, you can't force it on them.

It took me a long time to understand that not everyone wants to be better. Some people are content staying stuck in their ways. You have to let that go.

You can't make someone want to be better. They have to want it for themselves.

Your job is to focus on yourself — on your own healing, your self-awareness, that inner voice that tells you, "Something needs to change." When you decide to break free, to take control, to become better, it's one of the most liberating, powerful feelings in the world.

The day I decided I would no longer chase my abusive father's love, the day I quit my job and refused to take any more crap, the day I said no to yet another unhealthy relationship — that was when I felt the most in control, the most free.

That is POWER.

GIVE YOURSELF PERMISSION TO LET THIS POWER IN.

Never apologize for who you are or how you choose to express your identity! Your power is in your identity, in how you express it and live it! So, let it be free! You'll probably inspire someone else to ignite their own true self, too.

"No one will ever take you seriously or want to work with you in this city! ...And, especially with that hair!!" said the CEO of one of the last agencies I worked at in Dubai. I stepped outside and sat in a garden, tears streaming down my face. I knew this was the end — not just the end of my two years at that agency as Head of Social Media, but the end of a decade-long career in the agency world. Right there and then, even though I had no idea what lay on the other side, I knew one thing for sure: it was going to be so much better than the negative situation I was in.

Those words were like the 'Instagram post' I didn't know I was looking for! Sometimes, insults can be the best motivation. Take them just as you would those fancy Instagram inspirational quotes. They work even better! Don't spend time wallowing or feeling sorry for yourself. Prove them wrong.

That night, I was on Skype with my mum. She had just lost her job, so we were both out of work. I remember telling her, "This is it. I don't want to work for anyone else anymore. But what if no one wants to work with me now that my name isn't under a big agency?" I was scared, tears running down my face. My mum was the first to believe in me. She smiled, so relaxed, and said, "You always find a way. You always find work. I'm not one bit worried."

The next day, in February 2016, I handed in my resignation. Sitting in that garden, I remembered my Nana's words: "Whatever you do, be happy while doing it! Strive to be the happiest version of yourself." Words I still live by every single day.

CHAPTER 2

How to Find Your Way When You're Lost

Are you lost, or have you ever been lost? That period of my life turned out to be the key that unlocked everything else. This happened right after my New York dream came crashing down. Just when I thought I was at the top of the world, basking in comfort, BAM — it all got snatched away!

Trust me, if you're feeling lost, it might just be the best thing happening to you right now — but only if you make use of this time. There are real, practical things you can do. I was lost for about three years, and I squeezed every drop of learning from that time. I'm going to share it all with you, and despite everyone's judgment, I followed my gut. And thank God I did because it's gotten me this far!

Example scenarios you might be experiencing if you are feeling lost:

- You have no clue what career you want to pursue.
- You lost your job and aren't sure what's next.
- You're starting to realize you don't love what you're doing.
- You can't afford to study right now.
- You want to be an entrepreneur but aren't sure where to start.

My Nana was my light during childhood, and when I was utterly lost, she was the one who kicked me in the butt! People often ask me, "How do you know what you're meant to do?" or tell me, "I don't know what to do." Society loves to push this toxic narrative that we should have everything figured out, but that's just unrealistic. We're expected to know in our 20s what to major in, what career path to take. Are you freaking kidding me?! Your 20s are the years when you're far less likely to know anything because, well, you're so damn young! Plus, the possibilities are endless. So how exactly are you supposed to have it all figured out?

And guess what? If you do know, that's fantastic! But the reality is, many people — not just in their 20s but in their 30s, 40s, and beyond — might not have a clue. And that's perfectly OK. Don't let it make you stand still. Keep moving forward.

Society obsesses over IQ, degrees, and measuring intelligence with certificates. But the future? It's all about real-world experience, especially in creative and digital spaces. If you're aiming to be a doctor or lawyer, sure, you need a degree. But in today's modern world, there are so many careers that don't require formal education. Real-world experience is priceless, especially if you're a creator or artist.

Let me be real: I don't have a degree in marketing, strategy, or business. Did I feel like the underdog? Absolutely. But that, funny enough, has been my edge over the years! (More on this later.) What did I do instead of getting a degree?

When I look back at my ten-plus years in agencies, that was my university! Each year, I moved from one agency to another, each with a different specialty. I was on a deep dive of learning, soaking up real-world experience. So, if you're reading this and wondering, "How do I get experience?" you need to get yourself into the places and spaces where people know more than you. Learn from them, gain experience, and yes, you may have to take pay cuts to get there, but trust me, it's a small price to pay.

What to do to gain real-world experience in the field you're interested in:

- Internships.
- Summer jobs.
- Weekend gigs.
- Freelance projects — charge a reduced fee and explain that you're just starting out.
- Find a mentor who can guide you.
- Follow experts who practice what they preach and learn from them!

A Quick Note on Mentors

- Make sure they have a proven track record in what they claim to know and do.
- Do they live a life that reflects their values and principles?
- Are your values aligned?
- Are they practitioners? Do they actually practice what they preach?
- Watch out for fakes. Do your homework on the person you're trusting and following.
- Avoid flip-flopping between too many mentors. You'll gain less clarity and end up more confused.

GO GET LOST

Let's go back to when my New York dream crashed, and I found myself back in Portugal. For the next three years, I was utterly lost. Not just lost, but with no sense of belonging. By the time I was 22, I had transformed myself to fit in the UK, learned to speak perfect Standard American English to fit in New York, and now, I was back in Portugal with no clue who I was.

When you have a crystal-clear idea of what you want, and then it's gone, it's tough to grasp what's next. I wanted that fire and passion back, but all I felt was emptiness. Yet, looking back, I can say: **being lost was one of the best things that happened to me**.

Being lost forces you to be more self-aware. I'm kind of weird because sometimes I wish I could get lost all over again. When you're lost, you end up discovering the most amazing things you'd never have found otherwise. You find yourself stumbling into moments of serendipity.

Most people are so focused on what their 'perfect life' should look like that they leave no room for the magic of "what if?" Being lost, or not being sure of your next step, is completely normal. In fact, I'd argue that it's essential! We evolve, we change, and we're fluid. We are not machines.

So, next time someone asks, just say: **"I'm figuring it out and trying out a ton of exciting stuff!"**

Practical Things to Do When You're Feeling Lost:

- Travel and explore new places — do it alone if you can.
- Pick up as many hobbies and activities as possible, even the crazy ones.
- Pay attention to the things you naturally gravitate towards in your free time.
- Make a list of things you find yourself enjoying during your downtime.
- Take up random jobs; weekend, summer, full-time, or part-time.
- What have you always been curious about? Go try it!
- Study. There are so many free courses and workshops out there.
- Become a practitioner. Theory will only get you so far — you've got to try things.
- Give yourself a timeline for experimenting, but don't overthink it.
- Avoid leaving your job without a backup plan.
- Be smart: if you can live with your parents and not pay rent, go for it! You can use that money to fund your experiences.
- Network and make new friends. Put yourself out there.

When I was in my 20s, I was lost, but I wasn't even conscious of it. My Nana played a huge role, both during this phase and when I was younger. We didn't have money for kindergarten, so my days were spent with her in the theater, surrounded by flamboyant, fabulous opera singers. She was a diva, and she lived in this parallel creative universe.

My Nana and her wild friends filled our tiny apartment with fantasy. We didn't have much, but she made sure it was a world of color and magic. They would play with my hair, spray it to the heavens, and do my makeup. Their fierce, bold ways came with empowering words that echoed in my ears, telling me to stand tall and be strong.

She kicked my butt one day and said, **"I don't know what you're going to do, but you need to get your ass out there and figure it out. You can start by getting a job instead of sitting in that dark room feeling sorry for yourself!"**

Everything that happened during those 'lost' years propelled me to where I am today.

If you're lost, know that this can be the best time for you, but only if you open yourself up to the challenge!

STREET SMARTS

During my lost years (or as I call them, my "WTF am I doing?" years), things were like a puzzle with pieces that just didn't fit. I launched myself into everything. I joined my mum in São Paulo, Brazil, lived there for a year, worked at the Hard Rock Café in Lisbon and London. I did this to sustain myself financially and learn everything I could about hospitality, even though I knew it wasn't my long-term career.

I met people who would later become my mentors. I was always driven to be the best—or at least one of the best—at whatever I did. Life came full circle when Hard Rock Café became one of my clients, and I got to provide them with social media training. I even spent two months crossing the Sahara Desert (seriously, if you ever get the chance, DO IT; it's a mind-blowing experience!). It might sound like a cliché, but there I was, sitting on a sand dune, gazing up at the Milky Way, enveloped by the most beautiful, serene silence I had ever known, and that's when it hit me. My next move: head back to London and study *something*. I didn't know what yet, but I knew I'd figure it out. That journey through the Sahara gave me clarity. Sometimes you have to remove yourself from your situation to see things clearly from afar and gain a new perspective.

Ever noticed how we get so caught up in our own little bubbles? You don't have to be as extreme as crossing the Sahara. Do something smaller—take a solo trip, hop on a train to a new city, drive to the coast. Go alone. Create that space to listen to your own thoughts.

Crossing the Sahara was also when I began to fall in love with Middle Eastern culture. The last day of our expedition ended in Tunisia, and I bawled my eyes out. My heart and soul did not want the journey to end. So, after that trip, I moved from Lisbon to London in 2006, thinking, "Hey, maybe I'll try journalism." It made perfect sense—communication, storytelling—after all, I was a natural communicator. But three months into a three-year diploma, I bailed. Yep, I dropped out. It just wasn't my thing. Grammar drills, rigid structure, and studying like that—it was suffocating. Some people thought I was nuts for leaving such a prestigious program, but it wasn't for me, and that was a huge win!

Maybe you've felt something similar? Or maybe you're in a situation where you're forcing yourself down a path that doesn't feel right? Listen, you know yourself better than anyone else. You've got to follow your heart, no matter what your friends, family, or society might say. Tune them out and carve your own path. **You have to get 'there' your way.**

Next, I tried a one-year diploma in Interior Design at the London College of Communication. Nope, I was NOT about to spend years slogging through a degree. My mum taught me that you can learn a lot more out in the real world, so my mindset was simple: pick up skills fast, then dive into real-world experiences. I was a mess when it came to AutoCAD, but I could present concepts and branding like nobody's business. So, I traded skills with a classmate: she handled my AutoCAD, and I helped her shine in presentations. Boom—win-win!

It was my tutor, Valery, who pulled me aside one day and said, "Alex, you kind of suck at AutoCAD, but you've got a natural flair for branding, tech, and this whole web marketing thing." Until that moment, I didn't even realize that my pastime—tinkering around with digital stuff—could be my future!

I loved learning about multimedia back then (yep, I'm talking early days of the internet!). I taught myself some HTML coding, played around with Adobe Dreamweaver, devoured every PC guide magazine, and spent countless hours on Myspace and Hi5, taking apart computers just for fun. But it hadn't dawned on me that this could be *my thing*.

Then, the pieces finally clicked! I asked Valery, "Is there a one-year course for this stuff?" She laughed, saying, "It's still so new… maybe next year." (Can you imagine? Nowadays, you can learn branding and digital marketing anywhere! I even built my Rebel Academy courses around this!). So, she suggested internships, and that's how it all began.

I dived into a few internships, and it felt like being a kid in a candy store. Suddenly, I was absorbing everything about advertising agency culture and branding. There I was, smack dab in the middle of the action… still a little lost, but soaking it all up like a sponge!

KEY TAKEAWAY: Pay close attention to what you naturally lean towards in your spare time. That's where the answers are hiding. It could be anything—activities, hobbies, things you're reading up on!

When you're trying out new things, ask yourself:

- What comes easily to you?
- What do you love doing, even if you're still building up your skills?

- What can you spend hours on without getting bored?
- What frustrates you or drags your mood down?
- If you could design your perfect day, what would it look like?
- Do you enjoy collaborating, leading, or managing teams?
- How long have you been dabbling in certain areas?

When you're feeling lost, **taste everything**. Try out as many things as you can. This is how I narrowed down my path. There's no "one right way," only the path that feels right for you.

It's not an exact science. A client once asked me, "Alex, I want to get into marketing. How do I know what I should focus on to get the perfect job?" Here's the truth: *you don't*. You've got to dive in, test things out, and see what resonates. If you're worried about making a "wrong" decision, just know this—there is no wrong way. They're all stepping stones, even if they eventually lead you somewhere else.

How do you know your favorite ice cream flavor? By trying a bunch, right? Same concept. You explore, you learn, and then you find your groove.

Some folks might not get it and might push you to "sort your life out." But don't shrink yourself to fit their expectations. That only leads to resentment and broken connections. Respect them, but make it clear that you have to follow your own truth.

When you live authentically, you might ruffle a few feathers—mostly from those who wish they had your courage. But you'll also attract a tribe that celebrates your journey and wants to see you thrive. They'll fuel you with positivity and push you forward.

Life isn't an IKEA manual! There's no step-by-step guide. And that's exactly why it's so exhilarating. Go ahead, get lost, experiment, and discover your path. Society's obsession with "having it all figured out" is not your problem. The most exciting discoveries often happen when you dare to wander off the beaten path.

BE THE UNDERDOG

My "master's degree"? It was those ten years jumping from agency to agency. My teachers? My mum, Gary Vee, some fantastic people I met along the way, and a mountain of strategy and marketing books. I'd hang out in Kinokuniya, snapping pictures of book pages (hey, I was saving money!). I absorbed every bit I could from branding agencies, media houses, traditional ad firms, to client-side gigs, all the way to Singapore. I was in deep, building my skills, learning everything I could. I said "YES" to everything, stayed late, took on extra projects, and shadowed anyone I could. I even recorded meetings, playing them back late at night, to catch every nugget of wisdom. Looking back, I was building my own curriculum. Feeling like an underdog pushed me to study harder, work longer, and stay hungry.

People would criticize, "Who changes jobs every year? That's career suicide!" But I knew it was my "university." Today, some still cling to old-school views that job-hopping is a red flag. My experience? Every interview turned out great because my diverse roles let me bring fresh perspectives. I'd picked up so much from each stop, it made me a more dynamic candidate.

Follow your gut. Because if you don't, and it flops, you'll regret it. But if you follow it, and it works, you'll have proof that you were right all along. Imagine if I'd listened to the naysayers. I wouldn't be sharing my story here with you today. So, trust your instincts—they know what's up.

Starting a Career in Social or Digital Marketing:

- **Learn.** Courses, tutorials, blogs—you name it.
- **Follow legit experts** who walk the talk.
- **Get hands-on.** Tinker with social media, content creation, community management.
- **Start small.** Take gigs, even if they're unpaid at first.
- **Explore everything.** From paid ads to content to strategy.

Create Your Own Opportunities:

- Work for free if it gets you in the door.
- Intern. Shadow people who inspire you.
- Use LinkedIn to connect with the pros.
- Take a lower-paying gig if it opens doors to what you really want.
- **Get creative.** Stand out. Show them why they need you.

Reminder: This applies to just about any career.

Don't underestimate the value of time, practice, and perseverance. Nothing great happens overnight. Working for free might sound crazy, but it can get you access to the right people. Look at DRock— he started out by offering his skills to Gary Vee, and now he's a top name in video editing. Connect on LinkedIn, reach out, and be bold.

Are you putting in the effort? Are you speaking up, being creative, and leaving a mark? If not, start today.

CHAPTER 3

The Perfect Day to Leap

Bootstrapping Guide

"OH, SHIT I'VE RESIGNED, NOW WHAT?!"

OK, let's fast forward to "oh shit, I've just handed in my resignation, now what?!" Today, I look back at the first and second years of building House of Social, and I can tell you that it was the real practical steps I took that made it all possible. Never underestimate practical strategy. Yes, you have your business plan, but next, you need to have a real and practical plan based on every realistic aspect of your life. After being on Skype with my mum and knowing that I would hand in my resignation the next day, the next few weeks were all about creating a new lean-machine plan for my life. I won't lie to you; I was a little nervous but equally excited! All I was, after being around so much politics, ego, working over-time, and taking bullshit orders, I knew that despite not knowing what the future held for me, it could only be better than the situation I was currently in.

If you are reading this and you're in a job that you truly hate, makes you miserable, your manager doesn't respect you, you see no growth, then please, please don't keep waiting.

Don't wait for that environment to change or for that manager to get fired, please understand it's up to you to make the change you are looking for. It took me a while to get this. So let me say it again, it's up to us to create the change we are looking for.

Too many people stay in a bad job situation and spend endless time complaining and waiting for things to change. You'll never know when or how that company will change. There are so many other aspects involved. Sadly, you might be the smallest fish, and yet you're still there waiting and waiting for change?

If a situation is really bad, the longer you stay, the worse it is for you. The longer you wait for that change, the more control of your life you are giving to other people.
Wait! Read that again! Please take action, don't sit idle and keep waking up miserable every morning, but still showing up at the job you hate.
You need to be in control of your choices, and guess what? 99% of the time, we all are, but we let fear kick in, insecurities crawl in. We are human, yes, but how much space do we give fear? Too much. And it's only because of scary uncertainty, the not knowing. Most people like security. They like 'safe.' Well, have I got some news for you! If you really want to give self-funding & entrepreneurship a go, all the security goes out of the window! In fact, you'll want to thrive on the not knowing. It will give you that edge, that excitement to make it work. Because you're all in!
For myself, I perform better under pressure, or chaos even though I'm also a good planner. I love sorting out my clients' problems and confusions, or when the students on my six-week program are figuring out their ideas, they are a little all over the place. I also love not knowing exactly where I'll be in a year. For me, it works. As long as I'm happy doing what I'm best at, remain open to the journey, and see where things take me, that's all that matters.
For you, you might want to know where you'll be in a year, and that's totally OK! With your business idea, stay open, stay present, stay ready to change, and pivot as needs be, but more on this later!

Things to Consider if You Are in a Really Shitty Job, Want to Move to a Better Job, and/or Want to Start Your Own Business

- Do you have any money saved?
- If not, start saving money from either your current job or a side hustle. If you stay at the shitty job to increase your savings, don't stay longer than needed. Stick it out until you have enough savings, then quit for a new/better job.
- You can quit right away if you have some money saved up. Spend your free time looking for a new job.
  (Check the resources section of this book for more on this.)

- If you have some money saved up, consider quitting and picking up some freelance gigs instead of going to a 9-5.
- If you have a business idea you want to start, but you still can't spend your 24/7 on it, you need to have a job that will allow you to pay for your super lean basic style of life, so you save as much as possible, and you'll need to spend your free time on developing your business idea.

I…took the plunge. I just quit. I had no money saved up at all, but I felt 1000% confident with my leap.
You have to feel it in your belly, in your bones, because this is not the best option. So, I only recommend going 'all in' taking this leap if you know that it is the right move for you deep in your mind and body. And…you'll know you won't need to ask around much for anyone's opinion.

BOOTSTRAPING & THE SMELL OF FREEDOM

Bootstrapping definition
boot·strap, boot·strap·ping, boot·strapped

Noun

- A means of advancing oneself or accomplishing something.

Adjective

- Relying entirely on one's efforts and resources.
- Self-generating or self-sustaining.

Bootstrapping is building a company from the ground up with little or no outside financial support.

It greeted me with so much excitement, energy, and emotions that I can't write it all in words! I felt invincible after handing in my resignation. Even though I had very little money saved in my bank account (very silly of me), I had an amazing salary and saved nothing. So please, **SAVE MONEY!** It will just help you so much more down the line! I was still living in a shared apartment; I had turned down a very high offer (of approximately 85K AED) from a competitor agency. At that point, no money could buy this taste of freedom. I was ready to take on Dubai, even though I felt like the smallest fish. But how was I going to do that...?

My first goals were straightforward and practical these can be for you too:

- Can I make money from the skills that I'm confident and good at?
- Can the money I make cover my basic living costs?
- Will people hire me now that I'm not under a big-name agency?
- How can I stay in the country now that I'm working for myself? How much are a license and visa?

Go back in time to 2016, and Dubai is not what is today in 2021 (or whatever point in the future that you're reading this book). Business licenses were all pretty much the same package, made for big companies and most international ones. There were no freelance license options like there are today.

After I handed in my resignation, I worked my last thirty days. I told a few people, not many though, in the industry that I was leaving. It really wasn't like, "oh, let me sit down and do some LinkedIn business dev!" hahaha...not at all. It was just such a big deal for me that I just told a few people during conversations. The phone started ringing and ringing, and suddenly I landed myself two projects. I said yes to the projects, but I still hadn't completed my last thirty days at the agency. I hardly had the time, but there was no way I was losing these chances! I vividly remember my lunchtimes working with my new clients. I was working like crazy! So much for "Oh, when I quit, I'll have some time to cool off from all this crazy!" I felt like I was juggling ten balls in the air!

My final salary all went to pay for the license and visa I needed to stay in Dubai, approximately 40K AED, so say hello to the first investment of my bootstrapping journey. I remember my stomach turning as I paid all this money just so I could stay in Dubai without certainty of anything. There was no website, no personal brand, no House of Social. It was just me and two clients that believed in me. I didn't hesitate to take this gamble. I took that leap; remember the leaps… Now let's see how I landed on the other side!

There was also no discussion or doubt that I was staying in Dubai. I think I vaguely remember saying to my mum, "yeah, I'm gonna stay and give it a shot!" I could have gone anywhere. I'm blessed I could have gone home to Portugal or to Brazil where my mum was… But no, I was a woman on a mission. I had to prove (to myself) that I could do it 100% on my own, with no funding, no loans, no backers, no angel investors, no boyfriend or husband to support me. For me, that's how I wanted to venture out on this journey. It feels right for me. I would never want to have to answer to investors and be at their mercy. I wouldn't want to raise capital. That's money you then need to make in profit and payback. Instead, I wanted an answer to the question, can I make money on my own? That just sounds so much more fun and 'sexy' to try! I just wanted to…try. When I was growing up, we didn't have much money; even though I was young, I realized that everything we had came from my mum working long and hard hours doing extra shifts and weekends. Food, winter clothes, etc. And any extras like that damn Game Boy that I wanted so much I would have to be patient and wait, and sometimes I just wouldn't have the stuff I wanted.
If I was going to taste freedom, I had to be all in! I had bought my 'ticket,' I had buckled up and felt like I had been shot into the air! That's really and truly how it felt for me for my entire year one.

You have to do it in a way that feels right for you and map your actions to your ambitions.

Also, consider doing it in a way that will give you a true understanding of your capabilities. Explore what I mean by this by asking yourself the following questions.

Questions to Reflect On:

- If your family is handing out money to you, how will you know what it's like to have to make money yourself? Will you have the same drive, the same hunger? I've seen enough to honestly tell you it's just not the same drive. When you know, realistically, that you are not making enough money, not enough to pay the bills at the end of the month, I promise you, everything changes.
- Do you really need an investor? Do you want a shortcut because you don't want to put in the time and work?
- Are you wanting to start big instead of building from the ground up because you want to show off?

Over the last five years, I've seen many people lose money, get into debt, or troublesome partnerships only because they had a sprint mindset, versus looking at entrepreneurship like a marathon. You need to find a balance between the micro and the macro, move fast and have a lot of patience because things take a lot of time and work. I learned this from Gary Vee, and when I found myself in that situation, his advice made total sense. And by the way, I'm still learning to be better at it. If you watch me on Tea with Gary Vee, you'll hear him tell me that I really need to go more into marathon mode. For example, when I opened the virtual doors to the free Rebel Academy, people messaged me asking, "So, is it working? Did you get tons more clients!?" If only things worked that way! I would say it was actually six to eight months before I really started seeing a positive impact on acquiring consultancy clients and the uptake of my paid program offerings.

Next on the Plan: A Complete Financial Audit of My Lifestyle and Bills.

My mum took the lead on this one, and I had to go into a super lean and low-cost financial plan. Living in Dubai (one of the world's most expensive cities) would be a real challenge for most people. Mentally, this was fine for me. I remember when I arrived in Dubai, in around 2008, my salary was 2,500 AED. My final salary, ten years later, was 35K AED.

This is a must: Have the lowest cost of living that you can manage.
Audit everything, cut all the fancy shit, sell shit, keep the basics.
(Head to the resource section at the end of this book for financial coaching support.)

NO ONE CARES ABOUT YOUR LOGO

I see many people get so caught up in choosing the right name for their business. With endless rounds of logo designs, spending too much time and money on details that, in today's marketing and content culture, barely impacts the success of your business. If you think about names like Uber or Zappier, or even Twitter, these names are not special. It's all about the brand building, impact, usability, and practicality that have made these companies well-known. I doubt you'll see people sitting in Starbucks talking about your logo (and if that happens, then wow, kudos!), if they are talking about your brand, it may be about a piece of content, how amazing the customer service was, how good the product is. Maybe they're chatting about the nice message they got from you when they tagged your business in an Instagram post. I want you to spend more of your time, energy, and money on strategies for building your community.

For example, getting your social media fans involved, surprised, and delighted is such a powerful underrated strategy. Don't get me wrong, I'm not saying a brand identity is not important. It absolutely is. My point is that it's easy to overthink it, spend way too much time and money on it. Move faster with this part of the process. Don't ask too many people for their opinions. Creativity is subjective; everyone will have their own taste. I love turquoise, hence my brand (and hair) color, but you may not be into it. But hopefully, what I do give you is value, and that's always the end goal.

I've been building brand identities, including my own House of Social, for more than 17+ years now. My absolute best advice is:

Stick to what you like

You're the one who will be living and breathing it. Choose the colors, textures, patterns, moods, vibes, typography, and art directions that you love.

These aspects will make your whole brand so much more 360∞ and holistic to you. More on this later! Around 2014, I was walking in Dubai Mall one day, and I spotted the restaurant, Social House, and I thought, oh…that is such a cool name! What if I reverse it to House of Social?! And that's how my business name came about. It was really that simple. I love the word 'house.' For me, it represents togetherness. Back then, I knew this would be vital to the value of my brand, and the word 'social' was a must. It really served as the umbrella for all that could fall under the business. But when I thought of a name, I didn't know I would launch my own business that was still far off in the distance. House of Social's official launch wasn't until October 19th, 2016.

If there's one thing I've learned over the years, through launching my own brand and working with so many others, it's vital to have a very clear idea of your business idea, as this will set you up with much success to come. Sounds so simple, right? Well, let me tell you, this is what I spend most of my consultancy time on. It also comes up a lot when I speak to my social media followers or academy students. More often than ever, I see people starting a business but without a crystal-clear business idea. When I ask about the details, it all starts to flip-flop. For example, someone will tell me, "My target audience is mums!"
I reply, "Great!" Then ask them, "And what type of mums? Single, married? What are they into? Do they work, stay at home? How many children? What's their lifestyle and spending habits?" Then they begin to draw a blank. But this is just one example; if I gave you them all, I'd be here forever.

During my time at the final agency I worked for, around 2014 and 2015, my vision for House of Social started to come together. It was very much about providing social media training because there still wasn't much of this available in Dubai's social media marketing at the time. It was a while before this type of service had taken off in Dubai. I would sit with one or two colleagues at lunchtime and tell them all about my vision (if you're reading this, you know who you are!). I had it all in my head; the vision, the spirit, the type of branding I wanted. But this was still so, so far away. For me, the concept of having my own business meant I had to have lots of money, even be rich… hahaha… That was truly a very uneducated point of view. Even though I had read how Tony Robbins and others had started, the concept of bootstrapping was not alive and kicking in my head yet. Maybe because, in Dubai at the time, this was also not yet part of the culture. So having my own business was such a faraway concept for me; I knew it would happen, but many, many moons away…

The bottom line is, I want to make sure you have a very clear and mapped-out business idea.

Before I launched House of Social, I spent 2014 and 2016 (while still working for an agency) mapping out and defining what I wanted House of Social to be about. I can tell you that in 2015, my plans for online courses were already mapped out, Masterclasses, Bootcamps.
Many things will start to unlock once you start your business and throughout your journey, but the clearer your vision is, the better your chances of success.
It certainly helped me a lot to actually sit down and flesh out my first business plan.

Tips for Fine-Tuning Your Initial Business Idea

- Have a clear idea of what you want your business idea to be.
- Your idea should not be complicated to explain to anyone.
- Who is your business for?
- What problem is it solving, and how?
- Who else is doing it, and how does yours set itself apart?

Action Items

1. Map out your business plan.
2. Create your brand identity.

HEAD TO THE FREE REBEL ACADEMY TO WATCH A CLASS OR COURSE TO LEARN MORE ABOUT THIS TOPIC

GO TO WWW.ALEXHOUSEOFSOCIAL.COM/FREEREBELACADEMY

Answer These Fun Questions to Get Your Creative Juices Flowing for Your Brand Identity

- If my brand was a song, what would it be?
- If my brand was a celebrity/famous person, who would it be?
- If my brand was a city/destination, what would it be?
- What would that other brand be if my brand was to hang out with another brand in a similar market?

Online Resources for Inspiration and Creative Ideas

- **Creative Market:** A website that's great for brand identity inspiration. It's full of templates you can purchase and adapt. You can also find a plethora of amazing designers there to hire.

For more on this, check the resources section of this book.

- **Pinterest:** An online platform ideal for capturing ideas and creating mood boards. Don't ignore the power of mood boards. They're great for anything you'll do. They help you get in that creative headspace and help you decide what your concept is about. This can be for almost anything, the bar decoration you need, the packaging design, to the key visual of your online courses! If you decide to work with a designer, your curated boards of images will give them an idea of the art and creative direction you would like.

A TRAFFIC LIGHT SYSTEM SO YOU DON'T BURN OUT

Very quickly, I began to feel like I was in a parallel world to my friends. Suddenly you find yourself not having all that extra time for gossip, chats on WhatsApp, and all the social gatherings. And not just that you don't have time, it all costs money. Also, you start to notice the conversations you do have with friends no longer align with the things you're now interested in and want to talk about. But it's no one's fault. You are just on different paths. So yes, it can get lonely.

About six months before this time, I had lost 10 kilos. My fitness transformation journey played a huge role during my first year of being an entrepreneur. It not only kept me sane but also taught me discipline. Training helps your brain health immensely, so whatever you do, make sure you take some sort of regular exercise. Eating healthy has a huge impact too, so look after what you eat. Junk food and long hours won't help you have a fresh mind for the next day. Part of self-funding is looking after your mind and body; you will be pushing yourself to the limit, and you'll want to be at your best. That means looking after your body's health.

Trust me, I learned this the hard way.
I think it was at the start of my second year as an entrepreneur or the tail end of the first year that my body crashed. I just pushed myself too much. Training at 6 am and working until 2 am. I was bound to break. It took almost a year, though…hahaha. I don't regret it, though; I've learned from it since then. I crashed in October 2020 after the relaunch of my free academy. I've set up a traffic light system that works for me.

You can create your own traffic light system based on mine.
The objective is: To create an alert system in your head for when you are in go-go mode.

For me, this is when I feel like I'm on a high, and I can go for months working many hours, juggling a lot of projects, all at once. Because I really enjoy these highs, I'll forget to stop, pause, or even slow down. This is when you'll probably crash because you're not aware of signals your body is sending telling you to slow down, stop, or practice self-care. You are on auto-pilot.

Step 1: Decide your traffic light colors.
My traffic light system consists of only two alert colors; orange and burnt orange. You want to avoid red, obviously!

Step 2: Create a very clear list of the characteristics you display when you start to get to orange?
For example, I start to lose patience for particular things, and these things are very specific. I'll also find myself exhaling a lot of air like a long fed-up gasp, and there's more.
So, now you have clearly identified which signs your body and personality start to display when you're hitting burnt orange, you'll know when to push the breaks aka slow down.

Step 3: Plan what to do when you need to push the breaks.
Pushing the breaks can mean different things for you and me, but it is self-care and the time out we need. So, make sure you know exactly what you need to recharge, refuel, and re-nourish.

You'll be back to green, and you can go at it again! In five years, I've been fortunate to have only crashed twice. The second time was around November in 2020. It was not fun. I didn't want to get out of bed. It took me a while to get back up from that one; I had basically been on one of my highs since January, all the way through to October, doing eighty-hour weeks. Yikes!

The more self-aware you are and know your body's machine, the better you can 'drive' it.

FROM FREELANCER TO BUILDING A BRAND

One day in May, just a few months after I resigned in March, I was walking home late from the Starbucks that's across the street from where I lived. I would work long hours at Starbucks, picking up projects as a consultant, making more or less the same money as my last salary…

But guess what? There was no social media content, no "let's build a personal brand," zero…nada! Did I know about it? Oh yes, by now, I had read Gary Vee's books, especially the one about cashing in on your passion *(check out the resources section).* In theory, it was all in my head. But these past three months, since I had quit, had been about that list of goals, remember?

Would people trust me, would they hire me? Would they pay me, and would they be happy with the work I delivered? Also, I needed fast cash flow, so there was no bandwidth to create content at that time.

This brings me to an important point.

Please, be realistic. If you need money to pay your rent and bills, you need a job or side hustle to cover this.

Let's go back to that late-night walking home from Starbucks in Dubai's Jumeirah Beach Residence…I called my mum, she was in Brazil, and I said, "So… I've kinda been thinking it's been three months and I'm not doing bad, so… I can do this; I can launch House of Social!"

"Yeah, of course, you can!" she replied. And to be honest, that was it… that's when it clicked!

This was when I realized something really simple but yet so powerful. I was getting paid to do what I loved, what I'm good at, and not only that, I was doing it on my own terms, my own way, and I only had myself to account for the wins and losses. Most of all, I could pay my bills and have a little leftover to live 100% on my own. F* I had won! This was everything I wanted. This was freedom for me. Everything else was like icing on the cake, or sprinkles on a cupcake, or the cherry on top! For the first time, I felt like the sky was the limit! The fire in my belly lit up. And all of this just felt like fun, hard freaking work, but fun and so worth it! Every next move was clear in my head. I knew what I had to do, what it would look like. And trust me, there was no stopping me. When I think back to my first year as an entrepreneur, I treasure it so much, and I do want you to treasure yours. In some ways, at least for me, it was the easiest year. It's kinda 'easy' when it's the first of everything. There is no comparison to fall back on; growth is measured by what you get. It's really hard to keep doing the same thing repeatedly and then to grow financially.

So enjoy your first year, throw yourself in. The more you do, the more you'll learn. Innovate, pivot, and only keep moving forward!

To bootstrap, consider breaking down your big picture into small building blocks:

- Remove all the 'fat,' meaning: what's the 'leanest' practical plan? Example: Do you need to spend all that money on a logo?
- Start small and focused. Start selecting your superpower service/skill/product; this will help you stay focused, and you'll learn a lot.
- How quickly can you get your product or service to market and gain feedback? You want to spend more time getting it out into the market, as the market will answer a lot of your questions, and you'll gain the feedback that allows you to make improvements.
- Does it sell? Does it have appeal? What's the feedback?
- Have patience, lots of it.
- Create a business plan. I loved doing mine using the business canvas model.

Now was the time to come out into the world and launch House of Social. For me to teach and do consultancy, my way. To provide experiences that could inspire people when learning, I wanted fun, I wanted high energy, I wanted togetherness, laughs, and smiles. I wanted everyone to feel empowered, to do whatever they wanted, be an amazing marketer, entrepreneur, or side hustler!

I wanted House of Social to be a place you could come learn and feel the same fire I felt in my own belly. I feel that you could be and do anything. I wanted to be known, and I wanted clients to hire me so I could give them the best creative strategies in line with the current modern landscape because… I just knew I was good at my job. And…I really wanted to prove to people how wrong they were about me, that no matter how much they had tried to crush me, I was going to rise up, and they would see me. Could I do it? In a city where being an entrepreneur is a luxury sport? Would I stand a chance? If I could, then for how long?

IS BOOTSTRAPPING FOR YOU?

You have to find the answer for yourself. Yeap, that's right! Will it be liberating? Will you feel free? Hell yes! You don't have investors to answer to or key stakeholders breathing down your neck. It takes time and patience, and it's a marathon, but it's worth it! When I look back, if I had taken someone's money, I don't think I would have learned all this to pass on to you! I would have had it easy!

No amount of venture capital will fix a bad product, bad idea, by the way! In fact, it will take you longer to see that your product sucks because you keep getting rounds of money that will mask the problem. When you self-fund instead, you'll very quickly see what is working and what isn't, and you won't have a cushy money pillow to fall back on. If you are smart, you'll innovate faster, pivot, change, and grow!

Bootstrapping can also allow you to start while you are still at your job, then leave your job while you are building and growing it on the side! Is it possible? Yes, it is, it's damn hard but, again, worth it. I was recently on a Zoom call with the founder of Baby Palm Cakes, a vintage cake bakery. She had started baking as a side business to her banking job; it was her passion. Today, she is filled with backorders, has a waiting list, and is still at her 9-5 job. When we spoke, she told me how all of her free time is going into orders and her love for baking vintage cakes. She is also learning so much about the changes she has experienced and what she still wants to improve. I thought she would want to jump out of that 9-5, but she is being patient and still wants to improve a lot of the moving pieces before she goes all in! I love this real-life example.

If you have money saved up and you have made your financial plan, you can go all in and launch your business idea. You can also take the leap like me, be on a tight rope, and go for it to see what can happen! I thought at the time, and still, today, what really is the worst that can happen? I go back and look for a job doing what I do but, in an agency, or corporate job. That could be the worst-case scenario, and I promise you I told myself this over and over again when I was taking the leap. So, ask yourself: If you so desperately want to start your business or you want to change careers, what's the absolute worst that can happen?

Suppose you are seriously unhappy, miserable, in a toxic work environment, where you find your mental and emotional health deteriorating but have curiosity for something new. In that case, if you feel a fire in your belly to go off on your own because you have an idea you want to pursue, then take the leap. The journey that awaits you will lead you to so many experiences, learnings, opportunities, and people. You'll learn a ton about yourself too! Isn't that a journey worth taking to find your freedom and create the life you want?!

CHAPTER 4

Stuff They Don't Teach You at School – *Entrepreneurship Toolkit*

This is a marathon, not a sprint. Building something great that is profitable takes time. It sounds basic, but yet I'm constantly being expected to give magic quick formulas. I wish I had them. I'm sure many others would have them too. But building something great truly takes time; please know this.

You can make all the business plans, have the prettiest brand identity, have a new, lean financial lifestyle plan… But guess what? If your mindset is not right, no number of plans will make it work. It's the same as going to the gym, but you still continue to eat junk food…change won't happen.

Mindset Essentials of a Rebel

Practical optimism:
Meaning you're not going to say, "oh, whatever happens, happens." Or just being an optimist but then not doing anything practical about it.
No, this is delusional.

Being a practical optimist is how you will handle not just shitty, sticky situations but every other situation in between.

It's how you operate, how you look for solutions, ways out, and troubleshoot plan B or C. You will always look for the upside because, trust me, when you do, you're far more likely to find the solutions or answers you are looking for. **WHY?** Your mind is clear and wired for positive outcomes.

When you are negative, you are influencing your thoughts and perception of the world around you as negative; it will just be a dark, dark place…

Positive Energy:
We all have an energy frequency. You can tune yours up to vibrate more positively, especially if you have become self-aware of negative tendencies. Do you find yourself complaining a lot? Are you always judging what others are doing? Do you think about the things you need to do and hate them?

You can absolutely practice doing things to raise your energy levels and be more positive. This is so important; we all crave good, happy, positive vibes and love to be around people like that because they lift our spirits. But Rebels that want to build mini empires can't always depend on others for this.

Listen to music, dance in your house! Listen to a great podcast that makes you laugh or read stuff that inspires you. Watch videos that teach you cool, new stuff! Be around positive people. It will rub off on you! Make a list right now of things that fill your soul!

Patience:
The faster you want something, the more mistakes you'll be likely to make. It's OK to take longer to get there, or you'll end up taking the shortcuts that won't give you what you want. In the macro, as Gary Vee says, stay patient, give things their time, learn to breathe, and trust the process while putting in the hard work in the micro (the micro is the day-to-day things).

Discipline:
If you suck at this, I highly recommend you start to practice it. **WHY?** It's on those bad, shitty days that discipline helps you push through. However, the truth is, if you are doing what you love, even on the shitty days, you should still want to show up!

Practice the repetition of tasks or activities, that way, they become part of your 'fabric.' I was never an early riser when I started training and lost ten kilos. I started waking up at 6 am to train, and a few weeks later, I loved it. Discipline can mean many things, like getting up early, training, and learning. Work out what you need. For me, it's getting up early to train and work on my fitness.

Resilience:
For when you get knocked down, for when you got a "no," for when things didn't work out. For you to get back up and try again, and again. Without this, you'll quit too soon. Winners don't quit. They get back out there and fight.

You're not failing. You're learning and evolving:
You are learning and evolving as a human; how freaking powerful is that! How many people can say they have the courage to try new things, to feel and see other experiences and grow from them!

You have the power every time you make a decision:
There is power in making decisions, in moving forward. Be confident in making them and finding out if it was the best call to make. If it wasn't, you then know what other choices you have. It can be as simple as that. Stop the overthinking. It only sends you on a downward spiral. Go forth. Clarity only happens when you move forward.

Give, give, give and truly believe good things will happen:
It's as simple as that. For all the giving, I'm still thriving. I know in my heart good things will happen. Have I seen it happen in real life? Hell yeah! Just from my academy being open and free to enter, countless amazing things have happened! I will share some of them in the next chapter!

Karma is real and practical:
If you do good, good things come back to you. If you do bad, bad things can happen. This is real, no fluff or religion; it's pure logic if you think about it.

It can all end tomorrow, so live life:
Remember that it can all go away tomorrow. So seize the day and make it count. Life can be fragile.

There are no regrets, only moving forward:

Stop looking back on the past, on what could or should have been. My mum says it gets you a ticket to 'nowhere island.' NOTHING happens there. Why you wanna go there? You don't. So, stop worrying so much about the future.

2 OF THE MOST UNDERRATED BUSINESS SKILLS

Your gut instinct, I'm telling you this because listening to your gut instinct is a skill. It's a tactic. If you are an overthinker, need to have it all planned out, and have a huge sense of safety, then you won't hear your instinct or your inner voice. Loosen up, find quiet moments, find your center, and allow your instinct to help you. You have to train this habit, so it becomes part of your decision process and guidance. Many times, I find myself not rushing into a decision just to give myself a little time to listen to my instinct, and many times it has kicked in so fast! It will become second nature if you train it!

Simple Ways to Start Listening to Your Gut Instinct

- Pay attention to how your body feels and reacts to that particular thing. It's a physical feeling.
- Check your body language. Does it seem defensive, like it's retracting, open, or leaning in? Check your hand and arm movements, even how your legs are.
- Check your facial expressions. Do you frown, smile…?
- What does the sensation in your belly read to you? Butterflies? An immediate 'yes' or 'no'?
- In the first thirty seconds, speak what's on your mind out loud to yourself. What are your first thoughts?
- Practice spending quiet moments with yourself every day. Listen to your thoughts, clear your mind, focus on your breathing until you feel at peace and all you have is your breathing. Maybe a calm song or the sound of the ocean. Practice this daily.
- When you wake up, check in with yourself. How are you feeling at that time in the morning? What are you looking forward to the most today? Anything making you feel sad or anxious?

- When the day ends, check back in with yourself. Ask yourself how your day was? Don't beat yourself up! No! Be kind, be supportive, be positive.

In the future, when you are in a situation, start to practice paying attention to your physical reactions, to the feeling in your belly, and register your first thoughts.

Learn to trust yourself and give power to your instinct.
It can become one of your most powerful assets. But it will only work if you trust yourself. That's the key!

Working on Your Self-Awareness Will Be the Superpower to Set You Up for Success!
This will only equip you for success. Learn your strengths and weaknesses. What jobs can you take? What are you good at? What are you not? You need to actively work on this. I've seen disasters happen with projects because the person was not aware of this ability to deliver. Not only can this cause huge problems for both sides, a lot of problems can be avoided when we work on our self-awareness to know what to take on or not. Self-awareness is something that we work on forever. Make a list, write it down.

Bootstrapping Checklist

- How much money do you have to get started? Will you sell stuff/save up/borrow a little to start?
- Create a low-cost living lifestyle. Cut out all the unnecessary stuff.
- Make a new financial plan for your living expenses.
- Check all your visa costs and plan for this depending on where you are in the world or where you want to move to.
- Dedicate all of your time to making it happen, either full-time, after work, or on weekends.
- What renting options do you have to make your living costs super low? You can consider things like moving back with parents to save up on rent.
- Have a clear picture of your idea.

- Flesh out your business plan.
- Deconstruct your place of business into small building blocks.
- What are the starter essentials for your idea to hit the market? Decide your marketing needs, branding, and web presence.
- Make a financial cost of what you need for the starter essentials.
- Who can help you for free, or what can you offer in exchange for access/experience?
- What help/support do you absolutely need to make some of the elements happen? Consultant? Designer, etc.?

CHECK OUT THE BONUS CHAPTER:

20 Steps to Turn Your Passion into a Profitable Business

CHAPTER 5

Social Media Winning Creative Strategies - *My Blueprint*

In this chapter, I'm going to unpack a lot of the practical, creative strategies I've implemented over the past five years that have allowed my six-figure business to grow in revenue. Each year, my business is growing in a healthy, profitable way, with almost no dips or instances of not breaking even. This steady growth has allowed me to live a life I love, on my own terms, and you can do it too.

Want to understand more about profit, revenue, breaking even, raising capital, etc.? Head to my resource section!

Financial growth is the oxygen to any business, but for me, and maybe for you too, other elements play such a vital role. For me, it's about the type of legacy I want to leave behind; how much can I give to people for free, build a strong community of Rebels who empower one another, and ultimately, be the happiest I can be, doing what I love, filling my soul. And if that can be my source of income, I have freedom! I can't imagine a better way to 'win' in life than by doing what you love, getting paid for it, and doing it on your own terms most of the time! Perhaps this is you too.

In the following sections, I've tried to combine all the tactics I've used over these five years (and there is still so much more I want to do!). As I've mentioned before, this is not a book about how I did it. God, no! I cringe at the thought of that! It's a celebration of five years of bootstrapping House of Social—growing profit, scaling it, building a strong, engaged community, leveraging my personal brand, and doing it for most of the five years in a city where entrepreneurship feels like a luxury sport.

As well as my twelve years of experience as a digital and social media marketing practitioner, I've done a lot over the past five years, applying many tactics and creative ideas. All of these combined have helped me reach five years of profit.

So, if you want to know what I've done to get to this point, I'm going to share it with you. If you are familiar with my content, you may have some "ah-ha" moments and gain a more in-depth understanding of why I sometimes share certain advice. Because I've seen it play out and work for me, and I confidently know it can work for you.

Do I worry that it could all disappear tomorrow? Yes! Do I have moments when I think I know nothing? Yes! Hell yes! But I can't dwell too much on these thoughts. I need to keep moving forward, creating, doing, and showing up. That's the best advice I can give when you feel that way. We all have days like this. No one is invincible! So don't get caught up by what you see perfectly curated on social media!

Moving fast has been a huge contributor to my five-year growth, so please take note of this. The faster you move on certain things, the more answers you get, and the more you can enhance, learn, and adapt.

What does moving fast in the micro mean in business and marketing?

- Don't take a month to decide on what logo you want.
- Don't aim for perfection on anything. Are you 70% happy with it? Yes? Boom, then go! That's my tactic.
- Creativity is subjective, so don't ask a ton of people what they think about your key visual for an event, for example. Are you happy? Now put it out there and let your customers tell you.
- Don't overthink; stop that and make decisions. There's no wrong one. You'll find out the right one after you've picked one, so go forth.
- Allow the market to give you the answers you need. The quicker you put out a new product, service, or piece of content, the quicker you'll know.

Get the point? I look back now, and so many things I did and still do aren't 100% perfect, but I would rather push them out sooner rather than miss the time to strike! And on that note, let's briefly talk about this strategy: knowing when it's time to strike, or better yet, strike when it's hot!

Strike When It's Hot

In business and marketing, some things come down to timing!

Take a look at the classic real-time marketing tactic by Oreo during the 2013 Super Bowl power outage. They were literally at the forefront of real-time marketing by striking when the lights went out with the famous tweet, "You can still dunk in the dark." On another level, why are Super Bowl ads so powerful? Because, during those exact minutes, everyone is watching. When I got on "Tea with Gary Vee," as soon as it began, I started sending Twitter direct messages to the team asking how and when they would open up to international viewers. I got some replies telling me to keep my eyes peeled, and as soon as instructions came out, I was right there. That's very likely why I got picked. If I had come in much later, my chances would have been much slimmer.

Learning to strike at the right time takes a combination of skills. Some people are naturally attuned to it. If you think that's not you, now you know you need to be alert to the timing of things, and this will help you.

When things are 'hot,' there is buzz, chatter, and interest around that specific thing. Striking at that moment will yield a higher return than if there's no 'heat!'

Another closely related tactic to "striking when it's hot" is knowing when to "ride that wave."

This is another super-smart move. I had a few instances when we were in lockdown, and I started doing live mini-classes three times a week. After a few weeks, I felt a huge turning point in my brand and community. People were loving these classes, constantly writing to me with heartfelt feedback. They weren't just learning essential things; they were having fun, feeling positive, and looking forward to 6 pm. The same people showed up, never missing a session! I was on a 'high.' I knew I had to keep riding that wave and nourish it for as long as it made sense! In the end, I did more than a hundred episodes, all available on YouTube!

Learn to be alert and strike when it's hot to get the most out of an opportunity. And remember to ride that wave for as long as you see a 'high' from the engagement!

The Power of Collaboration

When I launched House of Social, I had my consultancy service, education programs, and Social Media Listening (aka Insights), which was another offering. I knew that a good collaboration with another brand could give both House of Social and myself leverage and awareness. Collaborations, when done well, can be a huge advantage to your brand, especially when both parties benefit. This is exactly what happened between me and Crimson Hexagon.

I pitched the idea of doing a Middle East consumer trends report. At the time, this was not widely available in the UAE or the Middle East, for that matter. Social Media Listening was still in its infancy compared to the US market. I love social media listening because it can uncover nuggets of insights that can impact your creative and strategic decisions. So, I pitched the idea to my friends at Crimson Hexagon in the UK, with whom I had developed a great relationship during my agency days, and had been using their platform. I could tell this collaboration would be beneficial for both of us. They needed to expand their market awareness and gain leads in the UAE, and I needed more exposure. Also, I had a team that could create the report in Arabic. After a few weeks of back and forth, with me hustling to ensure I had the Arabic support in place, I got a YES! This was a massive win! Not just for their trust, but to align House of Social with a brand like Crimson Hexagon, and for the final product we were going to produce! We were all equally excited!

Simply put, social media listening is the ability to monitor conversations happening online, from forums to social platforms. As long as these conversations happen on public pages, you can pick up this chatter. To further narrow this listening and uncover analytics and trends, you can pick up chatter by keywords associated with what you want to learn—specific brand mentions, for example. Brands regularly use this for customer service or brand alerts.

Brands use social listening for various purposes, like understanding consumer behavior, millennials' interests, problems people face, and feedback about products, which they can then use for product development. If you think no one is doing this, you're mistaken. For instance, a couple of years ago, I did some insights work for a famous makeup brand that wanted to develop a new product specifically for Saudi women. The brand learned so much about their beauty needs and rituals.

Listening to your community and the market is a huge skill— 'they' will tell you what is working.

Check out the Social Media Strategy Flagship Course on my FREE Rebel Academy and head to the Insights module. I unpack everything there for you!

After a few months of hard work, our teams—both in the UK doing the English listening, myself and my team doing the Arabic—had our Middle East Consumer Trends Report ready to launch!

We both got so much out of this partnership. In the early months, downloads hit more than 2,000, and this translated into leads, email contacts, and traffic for both our sites. The report was available on both our websites. I presented the report at countless marketing events in Dubai, met and networked with many people. Throughout this time, House of Social and I were getting noticed, even at the Mashable event in Egypt. Crimson Hexagon organized a special launch at the Burj Al Arab, which made for an exciting presentation in the main ballroom. One of the most exciting moments was getting on TV on the Dubai One prime-time news that night. There I was, with my blue hair and a blue background, talking about the Middle East trend report. I remember rushing back from the studio in Media City to watch it on TV, seeing my name "Alexandra Maia, CEO of House of Social," come up on the screen. I was excited, thinking how, only six months before, someone told me I'd be a nobody in Dubai city.

When you create a report or e-book, you need to think about how you will condense a big bulk of information into small, micro, bite-sized content that people can engage with, which leaves them wanting more and drives them to your website to download.

- This is creating a MACRO piece of content, from which you can create micro content for volume distribution.
- A MACRO piece of content could be an e-book, a report, a book, a long podcast episode, or a lengthy YouTube video. It has more depth and is usually longer or bigger in volume. It serves as content people seek for learning, utility, or inspiration.
- Versus MICRO. Micro is small, snackable content that is short and sweet.

HEAD TO THE FREE REBEL ACADEMY TO WATCH A CLASS OR COURSE TO LEARN MORE ABOUT THIS TOPIC

GO TO WWW.ALEXHOUSEOFSOCIAL.COM/FREEREBELACADEMY

Here is the list of assets we created for the report:

- The report itself was designed and structured to be easy to read, not long and boring.
- Promotional video, using cool cartoons, highlighting key stats from the report.
- We created more than fifty small pieces of social content that highlighted bits from the report and distributed them daily.

When I launched HOS, I focused on a few key things. Too often, when I work with clients, they want too much too soon. Yes, it's great to have ambition, but you need to focus on what your business needs at the present time. Concentrate on that, get it right, and then move forward.

Therefore, keep that ambitious fire in your belly but make it focused!

At the start of my first year, I focused on the following:

- **Building the brand.** When you build your brand, you create a world, an emotion, a movement, something that people feel connected to—a community. Common values are shared, and this is so powerful.
- **Making money!**
- **Being myself.** I changed from purple hair to what became my favorite color—teal hair. I stayed true to myself, even though in Dubai in 2016, when most business people, especially women, were wearing traditional corporate business attire, teal hair and jeans were a rebellious act.
- **Visually communicating.** My graphics were bold and colorful—teal, yellow, red—and I was a part of that. You may think this is normal, but in 2016, Dubai didn't have much of this style or way of thinking.
- **Giving free content.** My social media was filled with tips and real, practical information.
- **Vlogging.** I started vlogging because I knew that my face had to be out there so people would know who I was. Your face and personality carry more weight than a logo.
- **Focusing on key macro-objectives.**

Time to Put Yourself Out There

Part of building a brand is creating an emotional experience. A big part of what I wanted House of Social to represent was teaching social media marketing and discussing business in a simple, straightforward, easy-to-understand way that wouldn't be intimidating. I was tired of the same old stiff corporate stuff, complicated tutorials, and hotel conference rooms. No... I wanted it to be fun. I wanted people to come together, connect, make new friends, and learn complex things in a way that made sense. I wanted to create an emotion and a feeling that stays with you so that if you ever learn or work with me, you'll like it so much that you keep coming back! Whether working with me or consuming free content.

You want to ask yourself this:

- What feeling or emotion do you want people to have when they interact with your services, products, or whatever you are doing?

Ah... the butterflies! My first Masterclass 1.0 on Social Media Strategy was my first solo independent event, and I would try my best to create the experience I wanted House of Social to embody, within the budget I had. I hustled to find a venue that wasn't a hotel conference room; I wanted something cool and urban! If you're not familiar with Dubai or don't live there, you need to know that around 2016/17, hotel conference rooms were pretty much the only option. It has come a long way since then. Oh, hello to more roadblocks. The license plus visa costs had already been hard to swallow. I also needed event permits and licenses, which meant additional costs. I hustled for weeks until I found a super cool, urban venue that I could also brand.

In real life (IRL), events can be super powerful for your brand. Even now, five years later, I still get hired by people who attended my Masterclasses, Bootcamps, and workshops...

- Nothing is more powerful than bringing people together.
- It creates a sense of community.
- People will experience your brand, service, or product.
- They can walk away with an impact—whether that's a sensory experience, goodies, knowledge, or entertainment.
- You can host small meet-ups, gatherings at local coffee shops, or art galleries.
- Explore your neighborhood and look for collaborations! Maybe that new coffee shop down the road needs more exposure, and your event might help them! There you go!

You have a pitch for a collaboration that benefits both parties!

Below is a list of the marketing tactics I used and still use for my Masterclass and Bootcamp events that you can consider applying to your events:

- The most powerful one I can pass on to you from all the below tactics is **CREATE HYPE.** If you are not excited about what you are selling, how do you expect others to feel excited? You have to create the emotion you want others to feel. You can't just put out the content and hope people will buy.
- Create a **kick-ass short title** for the event.
- Create an **out-of-the-box graphic design,** a key visual, and assets to distribute the campaign awareness on all social channels.
- Be on as many social platforms as you can. **Contextualize the message;** don't just post the same thing everywhere.
- Create a **teaser phrase** to build curiosity.
- **Vlog** about it and show up personally on your socials.
- Offer **early bird prices** that already meet your bottom-line cost. By posting early bird, you are gaining more profit.
- **Direct message every single follower** on Instagram.
- **Direct message other people** on Instagram.
- Utilize **email marketing campaigns** and behavioral type campaigns.
- Make sure your **ticket-selling web page** gives all the reasons to come to the event, benefits, and outcomes. Provide a lot of detail.
- Invite **influential people.** I often invited people and didn't ask them to post online about it. Later, I invited influential people and asked if they could share. I never paid for these and was clear about it, so there was complete transparency.
- **Capture people's contacts** when they sign up for your event.

My first-ever event date was set, and tickets were ready to sell… YIKES, I was nervous… would anyone buy a ticket? Would anyone even come?? The day I went live selling the tickets, it felt like I had come out of the shower with no towel on. There was my face on all the Masterclass 1.0 campaign assets, there was no hiding. This was it. I remember being in a taxi on Sheikh Zayed Road, seeing all the big buildings, thinking of all the big agencies, and really feeling like a small fish. I just thought to myself, "Oh shit, Alex, what have you done now? Hahaha!" Will anyone even come? If you're putting yourself out there, maybe for your first Live on Facebook or an in-person event, it's normal to feel a little nervous! But hey, remember at least you are doing it! More than what a lot of people are doing...!

A client said to me recently, "Oh, but Alex, it's easier for you to do events. You have so many followers!" When I did my first Masterclass 1.0, approximately four months after launching House of Social, I think I had just over 1,000 Instagram followers. That didn't stop me, and it shouldn't stop you either.

When I launched, I didn't obsess about my Instagram followers or think this was the only place I could leverage from. My tactics were, and still are, 360 degrees. Maybe if I had solely focused on Instagram, I would have more than 35K followers by now, but I find it much more powerful to have more than one social platform with followers. Today, I love my email list that has more than 5k emails, all acquired organically. My Instagram community is super powerful. My podcast, The Free Rebel Academy, at the time of writing this book had reached 5k students! My FB Group, LinkedIn followers, YouTube channel. And soon, I really want to get a Discord channel going and focus a lot more on my TikTok game.

Don't become too obsessed with one social platform when you start. It's vulnerable to do that. Platforms are always changing.

You don't want to be fully at the mercy of their changes and algorithm updates. If we learned anything from the most recent FB family of apps blackout, it was exactly this! So... Expand & Stop obsessing about only one platform!

- When you start, **go more wide than narrow.** Be on more than one platform, and if you can, try to be on as many that make sense for your business.
- **Don't judge a platform until you try!** You know how many times I get this: "Oh TikTok is not for my biz; there are no people in their 30's on it!?" – Head to TikTok now and search #30club; there's a whole huge niche on the platform!
- Over time, you can start going into more depth on some social platforms because you have been exploring the ones that work best. Maybe it totally paid off to create that Pinterest page with mood boards, and now you can double down on this platform.

To get your content plan going and learn about platform strategy, head to the resource section.

Give What You Hold Onto Most

For my first Masterclass to the public, I decided to share my Social Media Strategy blueprint (refer to the resource section of this book). It had taken me about ten years to put it together. I had used it to win many clients back in the agency days and used it for pitches. This was what I would share with everyone, for only $109 a ticket. I remember a really close friend saying, "Are you sure about this, Alex? This is like your framework. If you give this away, won't it hurt your business...?" But instinctively, I knew this was the right move, and in a city where hardly anyone was sharing this type of content, I believed that if I did the opposite and provided value—something real and practical—it could only work to my advantage in the long term.

When you're the one who is giving out the most value, you'll always have leverage. Remember this.

This mindset continues until today. Going the opposite of what everyone else is doing is a strength and has many advantages. Just look at many known successful entrepreneurs and learn their stories. By the way, this is a great piece of homework. From Richard Branson and what he did with the Virgin brand, Elon Musk's Tesla and going to space, or even Gary Vee opening an agency when he had no advertising background.

Back to my first Masterclass! Suddenly the tickets started coming in. I could not believe it. I remember hitting sixty-plus and jumping on top of a café table doing a happy dance. When the day came, we pulled up the garage door, and there was a queue of people. Loud music was playing, and people from all walks of life were there—from marketers to entrepreneurs, people who wanted to level up their social media skills. There was even a couple of young unicorn rebels!

They filled the whole space and sat on bright, colorful bean bags. I invested in merchandise: notebooks, stickers, and tote bags, so people would have a little something of House of Social to keep with them and write down all the notes they would take.

If you want a little glimpse of how the first Masterclass went, visit my House of Social YouTube channel, where there's a cool kick-ass video!

These are some of the Marketing tactics I use that you can consider too when running your events:

- Depending on my budget, I sometimes run **Paid Media Facebook and Instagram adverts** (when I started, my budget was too small). Or TikTok or Snapchat ads, which are performing really well right now (at the time of writing this book). Look out for updates inside my Free Rebel Academy!
- **Facebook Groups:** find relevant groups and post there.
- **Personally email, WhatsApp/message people,** past clients, friends, and your community!
- **Collaborate with food and drinks brands** or any other that are relevant to you.
- Consider **merchandise items** (notebooks, stickers, and totes). Things people can keep post your event.
- **Distribute flyers** where you can.
- Create a **campaign for your socials** that is structured by phases.
- **Create HUGE hype!**

Check out my FREE Masterclass "How to Put Together Marketing Campaigns" inside my FREE Rebel Academy for further learning.

The ninety-minute Masterclasses events continued for the following years, running every four or five months or so. Ticket prices were never very high; the aim was always to have as many people as possible know about House of Social and for me to learn about the market and their needs.

I wasn't making a crazy profit from these Masterclasses, taking into account the rental cost and all other costs. There was some money left, yes, but it wasn't a fortune. The consultancy was always the financial oxygen in the early years, allowing me to invest in these. I also started doing FREE meetups, covering mini-topics and Q&A. I hosted them during Ramadan and at Christmas time.

Investing in these events truly allowed me to understand what the market needed. So I went from 90-minute Masterclasses ➔ 1- & 2-Day Boot Camps ➔ Deep Dive Workshops (2 to 4 days) ➔ to my latest format, online-only, which I launched during COVID: my 6-Week Boss Up Your Digital Program, which ended up selling out in 2 weeks!

It plays to your advantage to try different formats—you'll get to experiment, learn what is working, and build from it!

The Importance of Taking Risks

Did you know these Masterclass events almost never happened? If it wasn't for deciding to take some risks and walking a very thin red line, they almost didn't see the light of day. If I was going to write this book and compile all I've learned so far to pass on to you, plus the tactics that have gotten me here, it's paramount I share with you the importance of taking risks in your entrepreneurial journey, especially when you are bootstrapping.

Boy, oh boy, so much of today's House of Social business still comes from people that attended these events. So yes, the risks I took are still paying off. For example, this year, I had the opportunity to train the whole Hard Rock Café's franchises. After having worked there in my early years as a bartender and House of Social, what an amazing full-circle story. How did it happen? One of the marketing managers saw me live in action in Dubai at one of my Bootcamps and knew I was the person to do it! This is just one example of so many that I have.

This path you are on is not a nine-to-five situation or a path that is all rolled out for you to walk on.

You have to forge the path you have to walk on, and more often than usual, that path you want to walk on has never been walked on before.

Hence, you need courage, tenacity, and risk-taking. Will you fall? For sure you will. Will all risks be worth it? Not always. But that is the price you pay to create something new for yourself. Please remember this and read it twice.

Self-assessment reminder: Do you feel you have been playing it safe lately with your business? If yes, set time apart, grab some wine or whatever floats your boat, and get brainstorming!

If I hadn't taken some risks back in 2017, I'm not sure House of Social would have grown the way it did, and the story would have most probably been very different. When I started, I had this idea that House of Social needed a physical building to 'make it'! I wanted it to be the first social media school in the UAE too. In 2016, there was no social media school, and trust me, I checked! I was so excited, although it didn't last long. I wanted House of Social to be the first, but as soon as I learned about the amount of money for rentals plus the license costs for an institute, that idea was very fast out the window. I implemented the method I shared earlier about building blocks and broke down my business plan into realistic ways of getting it off the ground, so I could, with patience, work towards my "big picture idea."

Another reason to start off with building blocks is that many things may change along the way for you. So give yourself this opportunity. To be on the offense and react to opportunities that are in front of you and strike!

I'm really glad I didn't end up opening that building for House of Social in Dubai because with COVID happening, I would now be in so much debt, and you would probably not even be reading this book! Did I totally kill this idea? Nope. But in the past five years, so many more things have now come to play that are even way more exciting than this!

So, stay open to your process changing & evolving!

I wanted to tell you the stories about the risks I took, but I can't! For obvious reasons. So I leave you with a very important reminder:

YOU HAVE GOT TO BE WILLING TO TAKE SOME RISKS. Risks you can afford to take.

It's part of the process. Risks can mean many things: betting on a group of people to work with you, investing money in developing a product, or moving cities or countries to launch your product or service. It can be anything that you have a gut feel you should do and want to take a chance on, and you will be willing to take the wins, losses, or consequences. Not blame anyone else but yourself no matter the outcome!

You have to feel it in your heart, in your bones, and in your soul. You can't hesitate; you have to stand firm with your decision. It's a personal decision for you to take, and when you do, there are high risks and others that are not so high.

If you are averse to taking risks and like to play it safe at all times, be mindful of this, as the entrepreneurial journey, especially when you bootstrap it, needs a player that is willing to take risks. Maybe it's not you, so maybe you need to bring someone with this attribute to your team. For example, I'm highly risk-driven, but I'm thankful for my mum, House of Social's Chief Finance Officer. She brings a great balance to the table to my very risk-driven nature with her more tactful, pragmatic nature but to give her credit, she has just the right amount of crazy and adventurous nature too!

Say More YES! Than No!

It's rewarding to say more yeses than noes in your early days. Take the lessons, the experiences, and the contacts you make. They will feed you with so much more confidence. When I speak to many entrepreneurs early in their journey, many lack confidence.

You can get this confidence by simply saying yes and experimenting with new things.

Experiment, try different ways of doing things, build upon what works, and innovate. Listen to everything people tell you, not just when they are with you but on social media comments and direct messages; they are all insights. The worst that can happen is that it won't work, so you learn how to pivot and innovate.

It will always be more constructive to know what didn't work than not doing anything at all.

So, stop being afraid, get out there, and get the answers you are looking for. Become best friends with negative responses. Learn to love them and not be afraid of getting them. Why am I saying this? You know how many times I heard, "Oh, but Alex, what if they say no?" I was told so many times and had obstacles in front of me that simply drove me crazy, but I just turned that into more perseverance to keep going and figure out other plans. You need to turn yourself into a "can do."

Many people don't know this, but in my first two years, I also experimented with taking on projects that were very much production agency model type. As part of their proposals, I was approached by agencies that did not offer Social Media but had kick-ass clients and wanted to sell it. These brands were international brands. I didn't want to say no because I wanted to see how it would feel to take them on. It was very clear in my head that House of Social would not operate like an agency. After twelve years in the agency world, I had no interest in staying in the same business model. But taking on these big production projects put me right back into an agency scenario. I had a small team, not freelancers. At the time in Dubai, it was hard to find freelancers because licenses were not around yet. So I worked with people hungry to make extra cash and were also talented and wanted to work on these brands.

After some good projects, good money, a few ups and downs, and headaches, I called it quits. It resulted in me doing a lot of what I was doing in the agency world; I hated it, and I was spending a lot of my time doing stuff that I hated. Nope, that was not why I launched House of Social.

I had to say many yeses to get to this conclusion. It could have gone another way too. But now I know, and I had a confirmation that the original direction of how I wanted HOS was going to make me happier! Remember you want to be HAPPY! That's the whole objective of this process aka journey you're in!

Today, I work with a small ecosystem of talented people. I call them my unicorns and bring them on board when clients need extras like branding, design, web build, and other things. Together we have developed a lot of cool work.

Key takeaways:

- In the early days, **say more yeses than noes.**
- Be in the business of **being open to experiences.** You'll learn and evolve not only in your business but as an entrepreneur.
- In your early days, you may feel **insecure.** You can build up your confidence by doing more and getting practical validation for your visions.

Get Dirty

So, let's talk about the dirty, messy stuff, the not-so-sexy side but the one I really recommend you embrace wholeheartedly. Messing up is good; it means you are doing more than most people. It means you are getting yourself out there, either with your personal brand, service, or your product. Of course, you'll make mistakes, especially when you start. The problem lies with what people do when they mess up. When they mess up or make a mistake, many people let that take a toll, they beat themselves up too much, and they judge themselves too harshly. They take all this and let it be an emotional state of mind for days, weeks, and at times, even months. This is worse than the mess up itself.

I view mess-ups and mistakes as blessings in disguise, lessons that we can learn from, practical ones about your business or idea. Most importantly, when you mess up, this should develop your self-awareness even more.

- What can I learn from this?
- How can I make sure this won't happen again?

- What new process can I put in place to avoid this happening again?
- What does this tell me about my strengths & weaknesses?

I still make mistakes; I just don't get so hard on myself. I take on full accountability; it's on me! Learn and move on fast! In my first or second year, one of my biggest mistakes was sending the director of a known agency a very rude email (with some very angry emojis to go with it, hahaha!) and telling him I was done with the project! BTW, it was a super cool project with a famous make-up brand. And if they wanted, they could go find another consultant! (I cringe just typing this again…trust me!) This was a fantastic opportunity at an early stage of my business to work as a consultant for a big agency on an international make-up brand.

At this time, I was still handling all of my financing, plus the payment process with clients, and there had been a lot of messy back and forth with an agency. They were messing me around a lot. However, while kicking off the project, trying to keep up with finance and the payment process, I misread one of the emails. I scanned it and read it too fast, so when Alex punched out a very fed-up email, I reached my ultimate limit. You have no idea how proud I was of myself. Are you laughing now? Because I was. I thought I had done a great thing, "Oh mum, look how I stuck up for myself!" I told my mum when I called her.

I had also forwarded her the email so she could read it for herself. My mum, on the other end of the line, waits for me to stop boasting about my proud move, and in a simple, calm tone, she asks me: "Hum... Did you read the whole email? Because it sounds like he is telling you that he has the cheque with the full payment on his desk as he sorted out the issue himself." What? I thought, "noooooo!" I could not believe what I was hearing because, by that time, I had already received a reply from him simply saying, "No worries, Alex, we will take your recommendation and find another consultant." His calm and civil response. I could have died. I double-checked the email, and my mum was right. The evidence was in front of me. At that moment, I wished I could have got a shovel and dug the biggest sand hole and stuck my head in it.

What did I do then? What my mum and Nana always taught me, was that your character and reputation are everything. I knew I had to apologize. The next morning, I took a deep breath and wrote an email doing just that. I also explained that I had lost my patience and didn't even read the email correctly in the midst of so much ping-ponging. I also said I would fully understand if they did not want to work with me again, but I was willing to start afresh. As it happens, they were too. On that day, I truly felt the taste of humility. Who are we if we only go around cheering for our wins? We should also have self-awareness for the times when we need to apologize and admit that we made a mistake or that we are wrong.

Subsequently, I received one of the coolest emails ever. The director told me he was taken back by my apology, that it was refreshing, that he respected me for it, and that we could shake on it and get back to work. We went on to work on two other projects and became good colleagues. **Humility is strength.**

MISTAKES = INSIGHTS

I'm so thankful for this mistake. It allowed me to bring in a piece to my business that has allowed me to scale. And we want to grow, right? So, mistakes big or small, if you can get to the lessons you take from them, you can then see the opportunities to evolve or innovate in ways it will make things better for you.

I realized I was not the best person to handle the Admin or Finance side of the business. Conclusion: I needed a Finance Manager, and no one is better at this than my mum, as it is something she had always done at her job. I can close the deals, get the projects, sell, build the brand, but I cannot organize the financial side of things. But she can! Boom!

Today I can confidently tell you that much of the growth and scalability of House of Social is due to having someone else handle the whole process. Mum taught me a lot during our regular finance meetings. She is the strongest asset I have in my team, and without her finance management, I would not be able to feel so free to stay focused on the lanes that are my strengths. **You need to have your finance books in a healthy, organized manner.** Either you are good at it, or you must have someone supporting you on this. Even if you are a freelancer, this goes for you too. If you're not having regular check-ins regarding your finance, you'll become totally unaware of your spending and what money you are making. This is rule number one. If you are an entrepreneur, especially self-funding, you must be fully aware of your money books status, sales, profits, costs, etc.!

I only learned this in my second year in business; up until then, I was doing everything. At the start, I thought I was invincible and could do it all, but if you want to grow and scale, you need a teamand the quicker you start to build one, the better chances of growing you will have.

REMINDER: The quicker you can focus on the things that you excel at, the quicker your business will be established, grow, and succeed. By building a team, no matter how small, you will make money to re-invest back into the business for sustained growth. More on this in Chapter Five.

Do you need finance coaching?

When I run my free Zoom classes, I offer a one-hour finance coaching session with my mum, Luke (her alias name for fun). She has sound financial experience, so if you feel you need some help, email her at Luke@alexhouseofsocial.com for your FREE coaching session to get you on the right track. There is no charge for this. My mum's real name is Fernanda Carvalho.

CHAPTER 6
How to Build a Kickass Brand

As I shared with you before, the educational events played a huge part in getting House of Social established in Dubai and getting people to have a taste of what I'm about. In 2016/17/18, the concept of social media consultancy was still relatively new compared to more mature markets such as the US or UK. Traditional advertising agencies were Dubai's main infrastructure versus social media consultants.

When it comes to building a brand, one key ingredient you want to always keep in mind is: How to get people to stay in your brand funnel and not leave, and even if they do, that they still come back. Keeping people in your brand funnel, aka the top of mind, has many advantages that I'll go deeper into.

I recently was at a park and met with a personal trainer who wanted to get more clients. He told me he was posting three times a week, and I explained that he was leaving an immense gap on the other four days for other personal trainers who have got their content game ON every day to come in and take all his potential clients. I told him he needs to ensure that it is him that the customers think about every day. This will happen if you do a good job at building a brand + a well-nourished brand funnel.

Building a brand requires time & investment. At times, I even leave money on the table, but that is what you do when you want to build brand. You have to be willing to invest money that you may not see a direct return on your investment right away. It's a long-term game. I remember my mum asking if we really needed notebooks and tote bags and stickers because it was so expensive. Today, five years later, I have people that kept the notebooks! Another time, a client told me they had a meeting with an agency, and she had my notebook with her. The agency said unpleasant things about me. I remembered saying at the time that meant the agency felt threatened by little me!

Key takeaway: If you want to build a brand, you've got to be ready to invest and have patience. Get creative, too, to figure out how you are adding value to the people you want to target!

The return on investment will come back in many ways. **Have PATIENCE.** It's not a quick game or a sprint even but more like a marathon. More on this later!

"But... What Is Branding, Alex?"

Close your eyes right now, and I want you to think and say out loud three of your favorite brands that you really freaking love. (Clothes, music, artists, anything!)

Done? Now ask yourself why you love them. You'll likely be thinking things like how it makes you feel, does it uplift you, make you feel more empowered or elevated, do you feel relatable to it, gives you confidence, solves problems you have in an amazing way you love. Does it give you an emotional or an intellectual experience that you desire and enjoy, gives you a story, or takes you into a narrative you enjoy and want to be a part of?

Simply put, it is a feeling or an emotion. To create feelings and emotions, you have to create something to spark that and keep it alive. **It's the soul. The vibration. The energy.**

Has this got you thinking about your branding? Yes?! Yay! More on this next...

Welcome to My Brand Funnel Methodology

The way I see my brand funnel is, people have three phases, and they will often move from one to another as their needs and life progress. My objective with creating a brand funnel is to never give people reasons to leave, or they might leave, but they keep coming back when they need something.

HEAD TO THE FREE REBEL ACADEMY TO WATCH A CLASS OR COURSE TO LEARN MORE ABOUT THIS TOPIC

GO TO WWW.ALEXHOUSEOFSOCIAL.COM/FREEREBELACADEMY

Brand Funnel Levels:

1. They are exploring.
2. They need practical help/value/to be entertained.

3. They are ready to buy/convert.

If you create consistent content in volume and distribute it in various forms across social platforms, you hit numbers one and two, which gives you high chances to hit number three.

If I managed to get on Forbes Middle East in my second year, it was down to brand building and all the other opportunities that followed. Like the full feature on Gulf Business, speaking at Mashable at Cairo in Egypt, on Social Media Day conference, and being asked to be on the radio regularly on Dubai Eye.

My content strategy has evolved massively, and that is because I don't overthink it or want it to be perfect.

You need to move fast with content to quickly learn what works and double down on that. Content is storytelling, and in 2021 and the following years to come, content is only going to become even more challenging. That is because we crave so much variety and creativity.

Everyone is pretty much doing the same tactics and on the same platforms, so creativity is your variable to succeed!

- So, stay creative, innovate, change your style, be aware of visual trends, and jump on them. Too many people say their content is not working. I ask, "When was the last time you tried a new style or format?"
- The more fluid you are with your content, the less you judge it, and the more you allow your community to judge it.
- The more content you put out, the faster you move to keep making it better. So, stop spending fifteen minutes overthinking if you should post—just post. Guess what? You can even post again in a few hours or another day.
- You don't get to judge it too much. Ultimately, the community is the one to tell you what works.
- When you experiment with your content, you unlock opportunities.

I've always been goofy. Two or three years in, I can't remember how it started except that I began making and sharing goofy-type content. Wow, the response was so great. I had no idea I would totally embrace this. It was so easy, plus it's who I really am!

Create content that is contextual to the platforms you are on. Respect that each has a nuance. Learn how to distribute content so you can have content in volume faster.

Nine Ways to Re-Purpose Content to Distribute

1. **Blog content:** Extract quotes to create visual posts or Instagram stories wallpapers.
2. **Blog content:** Extract small paragraphs, use them as a micro blog post on Instagram, and curate images from other sources or your own.
3. **Podcast:** Transcribe audio into a blog and publish them as LinkedIn articles.
4. **Video:** Rip and put the sound from the video to create podcast content.
5. **Long-form video:** Cut small clips to distribute across social.
6. **Images:** Use carousels to tell stories or share information/create Instagram stories wallpapers.
7. **Tweets:** Screenshot them and use them on Instagram posts.
8. **Clubhouse audio:** Use this for podcast episodes.
9. **Instagram stories:** Take your Instagram feed image, re-share it to your IG stories, and ask a question about it.

For more on how to re-purpose content:

HEAD TO THE FREE REBEL ACADEMY TO WATCH A CLASS OR COURSE TO LEARN MORE ABOUT THIS TOPIC

GO TO WWW.ALEXHOUSEOFSOCIAL.COM/FREEREBELACADEMY

Igniting Your Personal Brand & Community

Let me tell you, when I started, I was not fully aware or self-conscious that my personal story was something that had a lot of value. However, as I slowly started sharing snippets of it, I began to see that this was something people wanted to hear.

I would document quite a bit of what I was doing or what was coming. I still do this today. I believe this helps in the community because people feel they are part of what you are doing when you start creating. They also see that it's not all perfect. My community has seen me cry, be frustrated, rant. I learned quickly that the more transparent, authentic, and vulnerable you are with your personal brand, the more relatable you become. In fact, the more authentic you are to all your quirks, the more powerful you stand a chance to attract the right people to you.

In a society and culture where everyone follows trends or tries to be like someone else, being your true, most unique self will pull the right people to your brand. You don't want to appeal to everyone; you want to appeal to people who vibe to your tune.

Sometimes you see a huge distance that starts to emerge between experts that you look up to so much. You see their content, and it's too perfect, too polished. After a while, it's hard to relate to that.

We develop relationships with people we feel we can relate to. Your authenticity + vulnerability + owning in on all your truths + (you are multi-dimensional; you can be a foodie and a skater girl, and yes, it should all be on the same IG page!) + your story is what will set you apart from all the rest!

This is for anyone wanting to leverage their personal brand, and you don't need to be an entrepreneur; you could have any job, C-level. It will always play to your advantage.

At the time of writing this book, the current pulse on culture and social media is all about breaking free from that perfect, polished image and embracing diversity and equality. All body sizes are being celebrated, with everyday people and brands getting on board to celebrate all bodies. Gender diversity and equality are being honored and talked about more and more. Activism is a huge one. And these are just to name a few. I'm excited about the future. So when I tell you to embrace your quirks, please do. Either you bake vampire-themed cakes, start learning to play the piano, or you have opinions you want to share with the world. Whatever your quirks are, there is a niche that appeals to a whole bunch of people out there.

My personal brand journey also evolved over the years and continues. In the first few years, I was not sure how crazy I could be, I started playing around with my goofy side, sharing my own journey, and it turns out that the type of content people value a lot.

My Personal Brand Guiding Principles for anyone from any niche, who is starting out OR feels their personal brand is not growing:

- **You want to start on a platform you feel comfortable with.** Do you love to write? Make art? Vlog? Start where it feels easy!
- **Format:** How easy is it for you to communicate or do art, dancing, writing, filming, blogging, cooking? There is no right or wrong way to do these things. Just decide. It does not have to be one way; a variety of ways is even better.
- **Content:** No content, no oxygen. Everything is about you. Your mission, your story, your journey, whatever you want to put out there. Content needs to be consistent, so show up daily!
- **Document:** This is always on, but more so when you are not sure yet about your content structure.
- **Inspiration:** Inspiration can be great, even if it only serves you to feel inspired. Do not go into comparison mode but follow other pages that have something to do with what you care about; it can help you draw inspiration.
- **Ask questions/share:** Make sure your tone is also very conversational. Are you asking questions? Are you sharing and then wanting to hear from your community too? Are you being inclusive of them?
- **Get scrappy:** At the start, it will not be perfect. It never is. But at the start, be OK with your content being scrappy. As time goes on and you get the hang of it, you will make it better or even get help with content editing.
- **Have conversations:** Not just in the comments but also through direct messages.
- **Small numbers, so what?!** Small numbers are great because it actually means you can give a ton of love to your people.
- **Pick a second platform to flirt with:** When you are starting, pick one main platform and one to flirt with. This is really important, so you are not just putting all your eggs in one basket even when you are starting.

Be in the service of your community; they are your lifeline!

- After all, if you want to provide value, you have to make it about them, not you. This is where many go wrong. They are being selfish about creating content, making it self-serving, and not experimenting enough to see what could work well.
- **My number one obsession has always been:**

- How am I giving value?
- Have I created content that I believe is best for them?
- Am I showing up with a mindset to entertain and provide value? (You need to define yours. You may not want to entertain, but be informational instead.)

Having a community, I truly believe, can be the most powerful thing. For me, I even see mine as extended family. They'll never truly know how much I love them, as I cannot fully put it into words.

A community can rally around you, learn from you, and be part of what you do. Share your beliefs and principles. They don't have to love all of you, by the way. They can buy from you, or they can be super fans. With no community, it would be like having a party, and no one is there.

"Your community sets the blueprint," said Gary Vee, and there is so much truth here. They tell you what content they like, what topics are more fired up than others, and if you learn to really listen in and reply AND STRATEGIZE and create based on these insights, you ARE WINNING! This is the formula to keep growing your community, maintaining, and nourishing it.

Make Sure You:

- **Get to know them.**
- Spend time on direct messages.
- Host Zooms/meetups/live content sessions.
- Have real conversations.
- Provide free access to what is valuable to them (you need to work that out). Ask if you don't know.
- **Surprise and delight.**

Your Most Powerful Asset Is...

Your story. It's the single most unique thing about you and what sets you apart from everyone else. It's what makes you memorable. It's what gets people to connect and relate to you. When you tell your story, you create space for others to do the same. They can feel less alone; for example, if someone hears you speak about your eating disorder, you can both now have a conversation. Because you shared something on social media, you both can share what you are going through. Let's imagine you have overcome this yourself, and you share your journey. You may have inspired someone out there in a massive way. They can have hope because you shared practical advice that they can consider.

When my clients or students ask me how they can stand apart or that they feel they are the same as everyone else, I always ask them, **"When was the last time you posted something about your story?"**

Elements of Your Story:

- Your 'why' and what got you to start.
- How you came up with ideas.
- The roadblocks you had.
- How you overcame any challenges.
- Fun moments about your journey.

Sharing & Communicating Your Story

- **Make your story part of your content strategy; make it a pillar or theme.**
- You can make one post a week about it or even make this your only content. This is great if you are still figuring things out; make it part of your personal brand.

Combining: **documenting your back story and the journey you're currently on** is one of the best strategies for anyone wanting to get started.

I did this so much in my first year, alongside my educational content with tips and tutorials.

Key Content Pillars for Anyone Wanting to Leverage Their Personal Brand:

- **Document.** This should always be done. Especially at the start when you are not sure what you want to be about, simply documenting is an amazing start.
- **Share your story.** The most unique, most powerful asset you have.
- **Share your point of view.**

For more on how to repurpose content:

HEAD TO THE FREE REBEL ACADEMY TO WATCH A CLASS OR COURSE TO LEARN MORE ABOUT THIS TOPIC

GO TO WWW.ALEXHOUSEOFSOCIAL.COM/FREEREBELACADEMY

A Turning Point

There was a turning point for my personal brand and the business in the year of the pandemic, or as Gary Vee put it, **"Alex 2.0!"** One attribute that contributed to this was:

Move Fast. I can't emphasize this enough. From all of the things that hopefully you'll take from this book, if you just want to take one for your business, take this:

Looking back at these years, I've realized that one key attribute for growth was I never got caught up in wanting things to be super perfect. Instead, I just did them. My first email template was not perfect, and my projector turned out to be super wonky during my first weekend workshop! **Moving fast in the micro things allows you to get out there to play and get dirty!** The quicker you are playing, the more you learn about the game, you practice, and the more you know about your people! Patience is your macro, and moving fast is your micro. They co-exist, and this balance is essential for you to create and have at all times.

Get comfortable with getting a little scrappy, unperfect. It's good!

Every day you can keep on working on making it better! When everyone left, and I realized that projector was not going to work, I ran out late at night and bought a huge TV to hang on the wall! The hardest part was seeing if people would buy my workshops!

Entrepreneurship is not a game you play by sitting on the sidelines. You have to get out there; even when you are not fully ready, play hard, get punched, get dirty, win and lose. Then repeat it all over again, every day! Take time out when you need it!

And remember, **you 'play' based on your ambition level.**

The first year of the pandemic and the months we were in lockdown were very profitable; what would take me two months to make, I made in a month. Something was happening to me at that time; I was so immersed in it, I couldn't put my finger on it, but I knew I was riding a wave, and I had to keep going! Also, I was luring this wave!

As soon as the lockdown started, I knew two things: **Live content would be big, and Facebook community groups would play a huge part.** I didn't keep this a secret. I went on Radio Dubai Eye and told everyone to start figuring out their live and community strategies, and I shared a ton of this on my socials.

The Mini Class with Alex on Instagram Live ended up with more than a hundred episodes by the time it paused! I was going live three times a week. I was just being myself, rocking up with wigs on, dancing, teaching all sorts of topics! I made little slides that would take me an hour to prep. I was teaching all sorts of topics and throwing a party all at once! They would go for two hours, three hours at times! I was also giving away parts of paid online academy courses, and people were going nuts for these! The response from the community was something I had never felt before… I couldn't understand it, but it was solely because I was just being me. I'll never forget one message from a lady saying, **"I look forward to 7 pm every day, it's the one thing that gets me through the day, and I think it's saving me from depression."** WHAT?! I was getting so many messages, and people were just so thankful for the classes, the information, and the energy. I was confused. I didn't get why this was a 'thing' now. This is who I am. Maybe it just had never been this obvious and compacted into such a short space of time. One day, my mum pointed out what I couldn't see; people were down and sad. And then there was Alex, crazy, filled with energy, dancing, teaching topics that many freelancers and small businesses needed at that time. We even did social media trivia! **It always pays off to be you, to self-express in all the ways it feels truest to you.**

Being you is the ultimate superpower. **Stop faking it, being someone you are not. Embrace all your quirks and your shyness.** Let's get real: there are people on social media, TikTok, or Instagram (for example), who build huge communities based on sipping noodles with ASMR sounds, creating miniature ceramic worlds, doing cactus design, illustrating on snow, and making yummy coffee drinks! There is an audience for everything!

Also, an important detail here; I did not have two thousand people watching. I think we were around a hundred or more, but it was the depth of the impact. **DEPTH is so important, more so than the big numbers people are looking to have.** In fact, BOTH are equally important; it's just that if you focus on creating a community based on impact, you may see slower growth. But instead, you are building a community based on care, love, and real impact.

How to Build an Engaged Community with Depth & Impact

This means you are doing all or some of the following, and because doing the below requires time and effort to win humans, people you care about, you may not grow in numbers so fast. But what you will be doing is focusing on nurturing who you have.

Nurturing the clients you already have will always have more advantages as you know what they need, and you can keep on providing more value in ways that work for them. Chances are, they will stay with you longer versus chasing cold leads. I always say start from the bottom of your sales funnels!

For more Sales Funnel Strategies:

HEAD TO THE FREE REBEL ACADEMY TO WATCH A CLASS OR COURSE TO LEARN MORE ABOUT THIS TOPIC

GO TO WWW.ALEXHOUSEOFSOCIAL.COM/FREEREBELACADEMY

Spend time on the DMs having actual, real conversations.

- **Engage in conversations in the comments sections.**
- **Do 'surprise & delights'** and gift your community.
- **Provide access to your community in various ways.**

Remember:

- **Move fast in the micro.**
- **Double down on yourself and what you are good at:** Showing up and hanging out with my community and giving them value (we talked about this before, right? So… put it into action).
- **Remain consistent:** People will take you seriously and feel they can trust you when they know that you keep coming back.

Apply these three at any given time, especially when you want to launch something new or draw the attention of your community to something in particular.

It's a Marathon, Not a Sprint

By this time, my online academy had been available for almost a year. The online academy almost didn't even happen. In a market like Dubai, where online learning was not huge, this was more of a test drive, and I just love to create and test things. Also, because I had so much content ready from all my events, I wanted to put it all online and be available anywhere and on-demand! So, in four weeks, I recorded it all, set up the site, did it all myself after work hours spent with clients, launched a paid subscription model, and to my surprise…people enrolled!

The price was super low, I think around $136, for three months, and there were other bundles, or you could pay month by month. I also had twice a month mentorship online sessions; these would be fired up to three or four hours with the students. I loved my online academy! But… I was losing money on it! The money I was making did not even cover the time I would stay on the mentor sessions doing Q&A, let alone my time and energy to market and sell it. Don't get me wrong, we had students; the conversion and numbers just weren't that high to make up for the investment. I read that people loved the online courses, but their time with me gave them the true value and impact they needed.

I remember one night having a chat with my mum, who then became my Chief Financial Officer (more on this in the next chapter), just blurting it out, **"I don't know, something is missing with this online academy. I know the product is good, but maybe we should give it all for free!"… but that would be too crazy…**

If you had told me it would be during a pandemic that I would fulfill my long-time dream of talking to Gary Vee and asking him for advice, I would have laughed in your face. But the universe knows what it's doing, and I believe in timing. The timing of getting on TEA WITH GARY VEE couldn't have been more right. I felt I was riding this wave, but was my online academy missing something? More than ever, people wanted to buy my energy, but how do I sell my energy?

These questions (not wrapped up in actual structured questions) are pretty much what you hear me asking him! And my very nervous face and fangirling only make me cringe! Watch the video on my YouTube channel; **www.youtube.com/c/HouseofSocial**

Gary simply told me I was making sprints by only giving half of my courses. I was only going halfway. If I provided free access, I would have a larger pool of people who would want access to me and who I am. This larger pool of people would want to hire me for consultancy because I provided so much value for free. This meant I would have even more leverage to charge a higher price for consultancy. If people wanted access to my so-called energy, they would have to pay a premium for that.

After releasing this book, the online academy (now called THE FREE REBEL ACADEMY) would have been free for a year. At the time of writing this book (Sep 2021), the Academy has 5K students, and the number keeps on increasing daily!

The Return on Investment of Free

My most asked questions are: Does FREE give you money? Does free work?

Even before making the academy free, I shared how making some of my events free has given me so much return on investment in the previous sections. I knew this methodology would work with the academy also, but to be honest, I've always gone into things that I've done free, with an open mindset, and open to the universe too. I believe that if you do good things, good things will happen to you. And you might be reading this, but it's true and works, and I won't be your only example. Look at Gary Vee; it has worked for him tremendously.

It's not instant. It takes time, so please be aware. But there are benefits, so if you want people to hire you, to work with you in whatever niche, for example, a yoga teacher, giving cooking lessons, selling art; whatever is your jam, you need to create ways that people can have access to you and what you do.

The more people have access to you and what you do, the more they get a 'taste' of what you have to offer. Also, the more you give in abundance, the more opportunities come back to you.

Therefore:

- **You provide value in return, and that creates an impact.**

- **Trust starts to happen.** People feel and experience that you can help them.
- **Credibility.** Because they get a taste of what you do, they can see that it works, or they just enjoy it. This is the catalyst; we go from the theory of your claims to them actually seeing it for themselves.
- **Continuous access to your service or product.** This helps you to stay on top of their mind. That's the difference between doing it with very little free access and not too often, to doing it consistently and giving it more volume.

You can watch my chat with Gary Vaynerchuk on TEA WITH GARY VEE on my Instagram or YouTube channel @alexhouseofsocial. Learn about Gary @garyvee.

This works whether you sell art or cupcakes, whether you are a fitness instructor, a book author, or a freelance photographer. When you are selling a product, especially consumer goods like food, if people don't taste what you have, they won't be able to decide if they want to buy it. The strategies for all of the above would be slightly different, but you do want as many people as possible to try food products. Therefore, sampling is ideal for this. Another option for consideration would be to create a mini-kit version of the product for selling or to give away as free samples.

You also need to be prepared to invest money in the free stuff that you go with. I have poured a lot of money into the FREE REBEL ACADEMY because I want people to have the best experience no matter what, and that is an extension of all that I do. So, if someone is watching a bad quality course content from me, that can negatively reflect on my consultancy. Therefore, you have to walk the walk and talk the talk.

Do good things and believe wholeheartedly that it will come back to you. All of this combined—the LIVE MINI CLASS WITH ALEX, making the academy free, the free Zoom live classes, and the ongoing free daily content—have all contributed to the pandemic year being my most profitable and the year after. In 2021, by half-year, I'd already made a total of all that I made in 2020 as a whole.

So many other things have happened beyond making money. For example, today, my community and my clients are no longer just from the Middle East. We have people from Europe, Africa, Asia, Australia, and one market I never thought I would get: America.

I got an email from the Marketing Vice President from Mailchimp when he saw the FREE REBEL ACADEMY poster in Lisbon! What?! That was insane! I had paid 0.50 cents per poster to have them all around the streets of Lisbon. This so-called **UNDERPRICED attention paid off!** I hope this truly inspires you to see things from this perspective, that giving free access can benefit you immensely, and stop non-sense hardcore funnels that only make your community feel you are trapping them in.

"What is 'UNDERPRICED ATTENTION,' Alex?"

Simply put, it is when you do something that is low-cost but gets a lot of attention/awareness in return! Think about what underpriced attention opportunities you see around you?

How to Sell and Do It in a Way That Feels Right for Your Community

When it comes to selling and monetizing from your community, **do it transparently.** When I sell my six-week BOSS UP course, I sell, but when I'm giving my content for FREE, it really is free. The relationship is transparent. There is nothing worse than when you know you are enjoying something free, or someone is only giving you one thing with the hopes of a transaction right away, but you are feeling trapped in a sale that is coming. When you sell, you sell. When you give, you give.

Trapping people in hardcore sales funnels is a shortcut that will hardly give you any long-term results. Please read this twice!

Your community will appreciate this transparency versus them feeling you are trapping them in for your selfish goals.

If you have been holding back on selling, get out there and do it correctly and confidently.

Actions:

1. **CREATE A FREE CONTENT FUNNEL:** What is it that I can create that provides free value, in both MACRO & MICRO formats?
2. **CREATE YOUR SELLING PRODUCTS/SERVICES AND DEVELOP CAMPAIGNS TO SELL THEM:** Include things like early bird offers, VIP early access, waiting lists, flash sales, special promotions, and a good sales page that contains testimonials, small tasters, benefits, and outcomes.

IT'S A GOOD DAY TO BE A REBEL

Chapter 7

Swimming with Sharks with Kindness

OK, let me tell you, this is probably the section I've rewritten the most! Yep, that's right. I want to tell you all the stories, then I don't because that's reliving the past too much and giving these people too much page space! There are so many ugly, messy stories. They've all become lessons for me. I've had tears and a deep sense of hurt. But here's what I can say: not one of my achievements has come at the cost of betraying someone, lying, or walking all over them.

You can achieve all your goals without ever stepping on others.

My conscience is clear, and I sleep well at night. Can't say the same for some out there, haha! When you launch yourself into the wild waters of entrepreneurship, it might feel like you're swimming with sharks or a tiny fish in a vast ocean. But guess what? You get used to it, it's part of the environment, and over time, you get better at spotting those sharks and learning how to navigate those waters.

One thing this journey has shown me is people's true intent. TRUE INTENT NEVER LIES.

Be prepared—everyone from family, close friends, colleagues, business contacts, or even strangers will show you both the good and the bad. You'll start to notice who's there for you during the lows and highs, and who shows up only when they need something. Then, there are those who promise you the world when they want something from you, but the moment they don't need you anymore, or they get what they wanted, they disappear, along with all the promises they made. I've seen plenty of that.

You will see the selfish, ugly sides of people you never expected. It's truly revealing how people can show their true colors without even realizing it. I've learned not to have expectations of people. Yes, it's hard because we naturally tend to have them. But if this resonates with you, start practicing now. Even after many bites, I'm still not fully guarded. But I prefer to trust and see what people do with it.

101

That way, I see their true intent. I'm an eternal optimist; I always want to see the best in people. In my 20s, this attitude brought a lot of disappointment, and sometimes it still does. But now, I keep my expectations real low to avoid disappointment. It's not easy, but it's liberating.

Having expectations from people almost makes you a prisoner of their actions that you have no control over.

In these past five years, there have been moments when I've felt like sharks were swimming right beside me, ready to bite. Let me tell you, there will be people who act like they want the best for you, only to betray, backstab, and even bully you. Can I give you an exact formula to keep them at bay? No. But I can share some ways to be more aware. Remember, when people attack you, it's rarely about you—it's a reflection of themselves. Often, it's their insecurity or jealousy. Of course, that doesn't excuse their actions, but know that you may have inadvertently triggered their unresolved issues, trauma, or pain. They probably want to take leaps just like you but haven't found the courage within themselves yet.

I remember an ex-colleague, unhappy at her job, saying to me a year after I launched House of Social, "You know, Alex, what you're doing and what you teach aren't really new or difficult; it's just you're doing it your way." At that moment, I thought it was a compliment, but walking home, something felt off. I realized that wasn't a kind comment. It was like she wanted to downplay my achievements to feel better about her situation.

You'll quickly notice how some people feel uncomfortable around you. They make condescending comments, try to be "funny," or mock you. Some will even distance themselves simply because your lives are too different. It's happened to me often, and it can feel sucky at first. It was all so comfy before, right? Shared lives, shared problems. But suddenly, you take a leap, and your courage triggers discomfort in others. Please understand, this has nothing to do with you. Your actions highlight issues they're struggling with, but it's not your responsibility to solve them. And never, ever let this stop your journey.

You are about to start building your mini-empire, so expect your life to change, and yes, you might outgrow certain relationships and lifestyles!

It's OK to outgrow friends. It's normal. My life has changed so much, and it still is. I don't have the bandwidth to keep up with regular weekend parties or social outings all the time. I don't have a huge social life, and I'm 100% OK with that. I don't even call them sacrifices; I LOVE what I do, so I don't mind spending time on it! Plus, I always check if my actions match my current ambitions. (And yes, you might need a month off! That's fine too.) Of course, there are moments of fear or, "Oh no, will anyone still want to work with me?"

On the first day of launching my business, I had a great welcoming! On October 19th, 2016, I posted on LinkedIn, sharing the news that I had launched House of Social. Within hours, an agency made a public post on LinkedIn with a graphic saying "FAKE." I laughed because it was the best compliment ever!

More recently, I was at a dinner party and decided to wear one of my wigs. A guy said, "Oh, you're Alex from House of Social, so you're still around, and people take you seriously with a wig?" I replied, "So seriously that Forbes Middle East interviewed me!" He looked even more confused, probably because I was 100% self-funded and making my own way. He then asked, "Can you explain your business model?" I just told him, "Go to alexhouseofsocial.com!"

I have many "sharky" stories from these five years. One, in particular, hurt deeply and took me about half a year to get over. It was the first time I'd been back-and-front-stabbed, involving someone very dear to me. I learned that some people promise the world and 'love bomb' you professionally, but with no actions to back it up. They'll start making demands under the guise of 'support.' They play the part well until they've extracted what they need from you, then betray you for their own gain. It's sad, but if anything, I feel sorry for them.

It's not just strangers; friends can betray you too—over money. But money can't buy real happiness or true friendships. People often want money to fill their egos, insecurities, or to show off. But ask them if they're truly happy. That's why I cherish my years in Brazil and the friends I made there! The Brazilians are amazing at simply being HAPPY! I've traveled to many countries and experienced different cultures, but nothing compares to the Brazilian spirit. They could lose their job today and still be in high spirits. Their optimism and positivity are on another level! They have such faith. It's an example to live by: always seeing the upside of life.

You can build the tallest building, you can find the pot of gold at the end of the rainbow, and you do not need to walk all over

people or betray them to do it.
Become great, build your legacy, hit your dreams and goals, but do it with integrity, kindness, and above all, remember: **YOUR REPUTATION IS YOUR CURRENCY.**

Thinking back to this particular "sharky" incident, it made me so angry, and I felt so hurt that I almost cried when talking about it. But it was a lesson I needed to learn. My mum said, "Better this happened now, still early, so your ability to sniff these sharks out gets better!" It has made me more guarded, yes, but that's OK.

Karma is real. Put good out into the world, and good will come back to you. If you put out bad, it will return sooner or later.

The more you believe this and practice it, the more the sharks lose their power. You'll start to feel lighter about these things. You learn to take the lesson, own any part you played in it, and move on. Recently, another "sharky" incident happened, but I moved on so fast. You learn to just **RISE UP, let karma do its magic, and move on.** You can absolutely give them a piece of your mind if it makes you feel better, but then move on. Don't dwell on it, and don't try to understand it.

Some people's self-awareness is so distant from themselves that you can't help them see it. It's not your responsibility, and you can't control it. **Focus on what you can control: YOURSELF AND YOUR MINDSET.**

Sadly, some of these sharks were men. I've had my fair share of condescending, misogynistic behaviour thrown my way. I hate to see it happen, but it still exists. Recently, a man I used to work with even body-shamed me on social media. It was disgusting. So to my dear male readers, if you see your male friends acting this way, do everyone a favor and call them out. Bullies, misogynists, and abusers need to be called out. Often, their behaviour continues because they aren't being challenged. When they are, change can start to happen. Women can feel more empowered to stand up when they see others do it too. The louder our voices, the stronger the message.

I wrote a blog post that went viral after a LinkedIn incident following my invitation to speak at the Dubai Police. You can read more on it: When Peter Ireland told me that having blue hair & wearing tight jeans is a bad idea in a Muslim country.

Sadly, I've also seen ugliness from women. It's already tough out there for women, and we should be supporting one another, rooting for each other. There's enough space for all of us. I've had women try to scare me with emails threatening to ruin my reputation. But together, we can create a stronger space for us all.

Key Principles I Live By Today, and Hopefully, They Will Help You Too:

- **Direct & clear communication:** Communication is key to any relationship, especially in business. Without it, misunderstandings happen, and assumptions lead to problems.
- **Trust but be aware:** I still choose to trust people until proven otherwise. I'm not disillusioned, just cautious.
- **Establish boundaries:** Don't be afraid to say no and stand your ground, no matter how much you're pressured.
- **Don't be hard on yourself but take responsibility:** Playing the victim won't get you anywhere. Own your part but don't beat yourself up.
- **Karma is real:** Don't waste time wishing ill on others. Focus on spreading positivity.
- **Quality over quantity:** Better to have a few real connections than many shallow ones.
- **Love your haters:** If you're not ruffling feathers, chances are you're playing it too safe.
- **Abundance:** There's enough for everyone. Don't hold back; share, give, and stay open-hearted.

I don't want you to feel discouraged by any of this. Your journey, depending on your ambitions, will be filled with beautiful moments, valuable lessons, and a few tough times. But it's how you tackle them that will make you a fighter and keep you moving forward.

If you face resistance, don't let it stop you. It means you're doing something right and evolving.

Please remember:

No matter what, take it on the chin, learn, grow smarter, and you'll always come back stronger. It might take time, but you'll keep moving forward, stronger and bolder. To forge the life you dream of, to chase those House of Social dreams, it's crucial to keep moving forward.

Winning Reminders:

- Obsess about giving as much free value as possible.
- Stay focused on a set of superpower services or products.
- Create storytelling content that sells.
- Understand your target audience's needs and how you can solve them.
- Listen at all times.
- Stay practical about decisions and be ready to pivot.
- Change and adapt. It's a sign of growth, not insecurity.
- Be creative and keep your content fresh.
- Let your brand evolve. Give it space to grow.
- Deconstruct big ideas and build from the basics.
- Embrace your quirks.
- Don't rely solely on one platform.
- Invest in the right tech foundations for long-term success.
- Create the hype. Don't wait for it to just happen.
- Don't overthink; let your market give you the answers.
- Surprise and delight your community.

HEAD TO THE FREE REBEL ACADEMY TO WATCH A CLASS OR COURSE TO LEARN MORE ABOUT THIS TOPIC

GO TO WWW.ALEXHOUSEOFSOCIAL.COM/FREEREBELACADEMY

Chapter 8

To Stand Out You Can't Be Trying to Fit In

If you're feeling the pressure, it means you're rising and growing. Don't they say, "diamonds are made under pressure"?

So, when you feel that pressure, remember it signifies growth, breakthroughs, and new directions. Isn't that amazing? Don't we all crave that—to find happiness, the things that make us smile, and give our lives purpose, deep in our souls?

Embrace every version of yourself and how you wish to express that.

You can begin at any point in your life, at any age. It's never too late. My turquoise hair represents my freedom, and the colors I play with are my way of expressing everything I'm experiencing.

Don't be afraid to be bold, to be different. The world needs all of us who rebel for happiness and self-expression. Our identity and the freedom to express are true superpowers!

Why do I believe the world needs more of this? Because when we strive to be our truest selves, we're at our happiest, at peace within, and that's when we wish the same for everyone else.

Negativity, toxicity, and selfishness fade away, replaced by the knowledge that there is abundance. Enough for everyone to 'win'! You'll be more inclined to share your story, inspire others, and help. And as we pass this on, others find their happiness too.

I remember being asked, "Alex, now that you're starting your business, you're going to change your hair back to normal, right?" 'Normal,' what is that? What society and culture dictate as normal? Should we conform to outdated traditions and viewpoints?

We must carry forward, breaking ground in new ways.

It's how we evolve. "Why can't turquoise be normal?" I replied. Was I judged? Probably, especially in Dubai. But I didn't care. And I say this not out of arrogance, but from a place of **confidence**.

If we're not living a life that feels true to us, then what are we doing?

Living a lie? No, thank you. In Dubai, at that time, being a Western woman with turquoise hair, launching a business solo, and discussing social media strategy was, let's say, a 'novelty.' I may have been early for the market, but that's OK. You learn to have patience. My mum always told me, "Better to be memorable than forgotten." And I believe that.

When you are a little different, a bit extra, or just shining brightly, you'll be memorable.

Remember Richard Branson's stunts when launching Virgin? He knew what he was doing, and it was part of his personality.

Your light might make others uncomfortable. You might be told to tone it down or fit an image society has carried for too long. **Never dim your light for someone else.** The right people will gravitate toward you. Those bothered by your light aren't meant to be in your circle.

Don't surround yourself with people who make you feel small.

Cut them out or create space. If it's family, be direct and share how their comments affect you. If nothing changes, create distance until they do. I learned this the hard way with my father, who tried to shame and belittle me. After years of trying to fix things, I had to step away.

The company we keep has a massive influence on our thoughts, behaviors, and what we do.

If you're ambitious and starting a side hustle, spending a lot of time with friends who just want to party won't help. I'm not saying cut them off, but maybe see them less. The people close to us impact our lives more than we realize.

Be around those who:

- Elevate you.
- Inspire you.
- Support you.
- Allow you to be your authentic self.
- Make you laugh, smile, and feel good.
- Have meaningful conversations with you.
- Are doing things you aspire to do.
- Teach you valuable lessons.

Create distance from those who:

- Have one-sided relationships.
- Constantly complain and bring negativity.
- Talk you out of your ideas.
- Make you feel like you're walking on eggshells.
- Seem to compete with you.
- Only talk about themselves.
- Only come around when they need something.
- Drain your energy or make you feel heavy.
- Disrespect your self-expression.
- Disregard your boundaries.

Boundaries are your best friends.

My mum always taught me about the importance of setting boundaries. She'd say, "People will only go as far as you let them." Trust me, people will push if you don't communicate your limits.

Make sure to establish boundaries, especially if you're a consultant or freelancer. Define your payment terms, your work process, and ensure everything is clear.

Essentials for effective boundaries:

- Never assume. Assumptions lead to mistakes.
- Double or triple-check everything.
- Better to over-communicate than under-communicate.
- Be clear and confident when stating your boundaries.
- Practice if it's new to you—don't expect people to know what you don't say.

Use high, positive energy when addressing uncomfortable issues:

- "I understand how you feel, but this is what works best for me."
- "This is the best I can do at this time."
- "I want to make sure I'm 100% clear on what you're asking."
- "I'd love to, but right now I can only do this."
- "I understand, but I hope you can see my side and respect my decision."

Always approach with empathy, clarity, and confidence, adding a touch of kindness and humor.

Growing Pains

Around my third or fourth year, I felt immense pressure. I knew I had to delegate more and stop doing everything myself. My relationship with Dubai hit a low point. I was frustrated by the costs of keeping my business going, and I knew things had to change.

Pay attention to how you feel as you grow. It's vital to make necessary adjustments.

The first year was the easiest. Everything was new—your first campaign, your first launch. But the real test comes later: Can you keep going, innovate, and pivot when needed?

If you're past your first year, you're probably feeling this too. It's a sign of growth and change.

A strong support system is essential. It can be a friend, a 'ride or die,' a spouse, a sibling, or like me, your mum. You need someone to call when things get tough. Someone to remind you that you've got this.

If you don't have someone close, find inspiration in others. Gary Vee has been my mentor for years, along with Richard Branson and others. I stick to a few core mentors for stability.

Rooting for Yourself Has Never Been So Sexy

Being your number one fan is your superpower. It's not about degrees or experience but the ability to support yourself.

Don't be hard on yourself. Don't judge, beat yourself up, or call yourself a failure. Instead, **be your best, loudest, and most amazing cheerleader!**

Remind yourself you're learning and evolving. No one is perfect; everyone experiences ups and downs. **Be kind to yourself.** You have to walk your path, and only you can do it with confidence and power.

Business Self-Care is a Real Thing

Bad days happen. It's OK. There's always tomorrow to reset. Need a break? Take it! Listen to yourself, then get back at it. Recently, a client told me she was exhausted and felt guilty for needing a holiday. I reminded her: **Your well-being comes first.** Without you, there is no business.

Scaling & Growing Your Business

One of my hardest lessons was learning to let go. As a 'doer,' it was tough to delegate. But to grow, you need a team. Invest in support and content production, build a micro team, and delegate tasks.

Consider these ideas for scaling:

- Create more revenue streams.
- Offer limited-time products or subscriptions.
- Partner with other brands.
- Create niche services or VIP specials.
- Produce online courses.
- Diversify with new products or B2B offerings.

Learn to Pivot

When the pandemic hit, I had to pivot quickly. I transitioned from in-person workshops to an online six-week program, which ended up selling out. **Believe in your product and have conviction.**

In difficult times, there are always opportunities.

Become a daily optimist. **See the upside, and you'll be ahead of everyone else.**

"Social Media is a Waste of Time!"

If you're a business owner or building a brand, know that social media is where real impact happens. If it feels overwhelming, hire people who understand it. **Don't miss out on huge opportunities due to personal judgment.**

A Siren Song to Dubai

People ask, why Dubai? Because there's something captivating about a city that rose from a desert. It's a place of opportunity and resilience. And though my journey here has been tough, the wins make it worth it.

I keep falling back in love with Dubai. It's been hard but rewarding, and I'm excited for the future.

Five years into my business, I feel like I'm just getting started. I wrote this book to honor the journey, but I don't feel like I've 'made it.'

Please know, things take time. No matter when you start, you have time.

If you're in your 20s, you have your whole life ahead of you! Stop stressing and explore!

In my 30s, I quit my job and started House of Social. I'm 39 now and more excited than ever for the future. If you're 40, 50, 60, or older, it's never too late to start something you love.

Don't have regrets. Live fully and seize every moment.

Any day is a good day to rebel and start doing what makes you happy.

I'm excited for you and me! We have so many adventures ahead. Never stop learning, listening, and expressing your truest self.

Vibrate your most positive energy. Happiness is the ultimate return on investment.

Live life on your terms. You've won.

Everything else is just the extra buttercream on the cupcake. So if you want to change your career, move, travel, or express yourself, **do it!**

- **Rebels are change agents.**
- **Rebels rise up, even after being knocked down.**
- **Rebels turn insecurities into superpowers.**
- **Rebels are kind, empathetic, and non-judgmental.**
- **Rebels listen to their needs—physical, emotional, and holistic.**
- **Rebels light the way for others.**

Remember:

Whenever you're hard on yourself, you're clipping your wings. Set yourself free.

Be the hero of your own story.

In a world that pushes conformity, be the rebel who lives the life you want.

CHAPTER 9

Going into Unchartered Waters

Raising Capital

About a year and a half ago, I was trying to fall asleep, and suddenly, I had this epiphany. I'm sure many of you can relate to those moments when an idea just hits you, but this one felt different. I sat up in bed, and it truly felt like the universe had given me this idea. It was as if the universe had planted it in my mind, and it sparkled with a special kind of stardust. I was amazed, and as I always do when something 'wow' happens, I grabbed my phone and called my mom. I didn't even look at the time—it could have been 4 AM or 3 AM, but that didn't matter. She is my sounding board, my partner in crime. That's just how our relationship is. Well, at least how I am—I'm an over-communicator, I love to share everything with her, even though she's quite different from me in that way.

So, I called her, and I think she was vaguely awake. It's all a bit fuzzy now because it was two, no, three years ago. From the moment I had the idea, which I remember being in early February or January, I called her and said, "Mom, I've got an idea, and I don't think it's like any of my other ideas. This one is freaking big, and I don't see anything like it on the market." She asked, "Okay, what is it?" And I said, "Listen up, Mom: small businesses in the UAE." She was like, "Okay, small businesses... what about them?" I went on, "Their biggest struggles are being discoverable and getting noticed. Shopping malls are packed with people, but small businesses can't get in because rents are so high—they're only for mainstream retail brands."

The biggest problem is that small businesses in Dubai struggle to get discovered. Another issue is that I don't believe they get celebrated and showcased like they do in other markets. There just aren't platforms that really shine a spotlight on them. These were the two main things I saw, and my mom just listened. Then I said, "We need to create the 'Etsy for the UAE.'" And she asked, "What's Etsy?"—I knew she'd ask that. I explained, "Etsy is an app built for small businesses and creators. The UAE doesn't have a dedicated app that's a marketplace where all small businesses can be easily discovered. Sure, there are some websites, but they're not very good. There's nothing like a dedicated app." As I was saying this, I could see it all in my head—the functionalities, the interface. I imagined people being able to save their favourite small businesses, get push notifications about new products, and how this app would do all the heavy lifting in marketing for them. It was like a local version of Talabat but for small businesses, or like Etsy where you can discover and favourite small businesses. It all came together in my mind, and I thought, "This is going to be amazing!"

I already knew what it takes to build an app. I had been part of that process before in the agency world, and I was fortunate to be part of the beta team for 'Hi Ho,' an app by Greg Spiralis and backed by Gary V. I learned so much about app development, retention, and everything that goes into a successful launch. I knew this wasn't something I could pull off overnight or in a month like some of my other projects. It needed to be polished, with an amazing interface and awesome features because the UAE market has high standards. I couldn't just create a basic, scrappy app. It had to be special. As I fleshed it out in my mind, a lot of questions popped up: Would we have e-commerce? Payment integrations? Delivery options? Suddenly, my mind was buzzing with ideas, and I could hardly sleep for days because I kept visualizing how incredible this app could be.

This was early in the year, and I waited until summer to really start working on it. The idea marinated in my head from January to around summertime, and during the summer, I dove deep into research. I explored any existing platforms in the region and found that there was really nothing substantial out there. The platforms that did exist were taking a huge cut from local small businesses, and as a small business owner myself, I know how tough it is to make a profit. It's already hard enough to make money, and then a platform comes along and takes a percentage of it. So, I kept learning throughout the summer, and it was clear that the way I wanted to build this platform was unique—we wouldn't take a cut from the small businesses. That was not going to be our business model.

I debated whether or not to share the name with you all, but you know what? I'll go ahead and tell you because there's a story behind it. Every project needs a name, even if it's just a placeholder. So, I thought, "What should I call this secret project?" And of course, turquoise is my color. Teal and turquoise are almost the same, so I decided to call it 'Teal.' That became the secret project name for my mobile app for small businesses—the Etsy of the UAE.

The business model was straightforward. We wouldn't take a cut from the businesses. Instead, it would be a membership model where they pay to be on the app, with different tiers offering different benefits, like consultancy time with me, advertising options, and more. That way, we could support small businesses without cutting into their revenue. During the summer, I dove into answering the big questions: Are people checking out? Are they purchasing through our app? What are the fees for payment integrations? There was so much to figure out, and I started mapping out a business plan. That's when things really started to take off.

When summer ended, I realized this was going to need serious funding. Building a kickass app, even for a beta phase or first-year rollout, required a solid budget, especially for a market like the UAE. Marketing here needs to be on point, and you need a budget to make a big splash. From the beginning, I knew this wasn't something I could fund on my own. I didn't have the savings, nor would it have been wise to dip into them. I needed investors or angel investors, and if you're wondering about the difference, I'll explain that later in the book.

After summer, I returned from Portugal and had dinner with a very close friend, who has now become an ex-best friend, but at that time, we had been friends for 22 years. Over dinner, I told him about my idea. He doesn't work in digital or small businesses, but he's smart and curious. He listened, and to my surprise, he said, "This is an amazing idea. I think you're onto something, and I'd like to invest and be a part of it." I was blown away! We scheduled a meeting for me to pitch it to him, and I realized I had to dive deeper into understanding how to work with investors.

Up to that point, I didn't know much about pitching to investors. What do they take? What do they get in return? I had to learn everything, but I quickly knew that I needed a solid financial plan. I worked with my accountant and my mom, who's a CFO. Crafting this plan was a whole new experience for me. To create a robust financial plan, especially for a big business idea, you have to flesh out your business model and revenue streams. Everything that goes into a financial plan depends on how you plan to monetize your idea. You can't just focus on the bells and whistles; you have to think through every detail of how the business will make money. That forms the base of your financial projections, which you'll need when pitching to investors.

A very exciting part of this journey was finding an amazing team to build the app. I spent almost three months connecting with agencies in Eastern Europe, which is known for having some of the best developers out there. I learned so much through this process, speaking to over 20 agencies. It was like a crash course in mobile app development. I'm not a CTO, but by the end of it, I had learned a lot. Every agency I spoke to was impressed by how much groundwork I had already done. Many said, "You've done so much of the work we usually charge clients for; we can skip almost a month's worth of preparation." That gave me so much confidence.

Finally, I shortlisted three agencies, and one stood out. Their team was so inspired by the project that they decided to quit their jobs, form their own agency, and take this on as their first big project. It was such an inspiring and humbling moment. If you're building something that involves technology, you need to find an amazing CTO, or at least surround yourself with experts who can guide you. I knew my strengths—I'm the brainchild, the marketing person, the one who knows how to make this work—but I'm not a technologist, and having experts on board is crucial for success.

By the end of 2021, or maybe it was early 2022, we had everything almost ready. The financial plan, the marketing plan, and the pitch deck were nearly complete. I even did a market research survey with my community, and the feedback was overwhelmingly positive. There was a clear white space in the market, and we had a solid plan to fill it. So, with all that in place, we were ready for the next step: finding investors and making this dream a reality.

This journey taught me so much, and I hope it inspires you to chase those ideas that keep you up at night. They might just be the ones that change everything.

WHERE'S THE PEOPLE WITH THE MONEY?

It was time to go ask for money. I was fresh. I was eager. I was ready. Asking for money was never a problem for me. My mom brought me up with the confidence to ask for what you want because, until you do, you've got nothing to lose. So, the asking for money, the pitching of the idea—that was in the bag for me. I was ready. It was like a race, like a Formula One track that I could see clearly. Well, no, okay, I'm going too far. I definitely did not see it. I didn't see it because... where are the people with the money?

Where are the investors, the people, or the angel investors, and where are they?

Where do they hang out? How do you go about finding them? And then, yeah, so all of that was really unclear.

Angel investors are your close friends, family members. Angel investors are people who really believe in you, and they are likely to already know you. So they know you as a person. They have some sort of relationship with you, proximity, and they are trusting in you, your character, your personality—sometimes even more than the idea itself. They can be early investors because they know you, and they believe in your idea. So, those angel investors were definitely the type of people I was looking for in the beginning. Now, my friend was an angel investor—the one I told you about in the previous chapter. He was a key investor, and he also became a huge key player with me in the mission to find the money. He definitely played his part really well. He was extremely good at the numbers. He was great at reading them. In fact, when we finished that huge, gigantic financial planning, he was really good at translating those numbers in a way that was more digestible and understandable for investors. So, I really advise you to have that person in your team, or, if it's not you, you need to find someone who can be really good with your numbers, someone who really understands how to present them in a way that's going to be appealing and attractive to investors. That was key.

You might have your monetization plan, you might have your marketing plan, but when it comes to your financing plan, it needs to be really locked in. And then, how you present it needs to be really attractive, digestible, and easy to grasp. That part was also new to me. He was great because he really took care of that.

But it was January, and I was ready. I was like, "Okay, let's go right now." We've got one angel investor, and now, where do I look for the people with money? Where do you go?

So, the journey began with diving into Google. Yeah, Google. I lost myself in the world of VCs, venture capitalist firms, investor circles, groups, even events. So, I really felt like I had to immerse myself in this world to understand what groups are out there, what events are happening, and where I should go. This was something I had never been a part of, nor had I ever wanted to be a part of.

A few people at the time used to say to me, "Oh, it must feel weird because you're going to ask for money, and you know, since you've been self-funded, maybe that feels strange." It really didn't. I looked at it in such a pragmatic, practical way. At the time, it was really like, "No, if we are going to do the right negotiations, I will always have full control. The shares and the way we're going to divide things up are not going to lead to me losing control. I'm okay." So that part was fine. I was ready.

The big question was: How do you find investors?

One of the first things I did was go on Google and search for investing venture capitalist firms. I pulled up a big list of agencies and companies in the UAE, and I went through every single one of them, sending out our pitch deck. This was new to me, as at this point, I was holding on very dearly to this idea. The thought of sending it to agencies and putting it out there was something I was a bit hesitant about, thinking, "Really? What if they take it? What if they steal it?" But I quickly realized that's just how the game is.

You have to create a 10-slide deck. My deck was definitely not 10 slides. So, I had to condense it. At this time, everybody was talking about this 10-slide deck. And, to be honest, I was speaking to only a very few people in my circle about what I was doing. That was something I had to get over, and I'll tell you more about that soon.

I spent days filling out forms and emailing a ton of venture capitalist firms in the UAE. I was like, "Okay, cool. This should hopefully get me some emails back, and we will go pitch, and we'll go meet these people." I sent out as many as I could, and that was a huge tick off the list. I thought, "Okay, well, that's done. Let's move on to the next thing, and hopefully, we'll hear back from these companies."

Then, I started getting into circles, like groups. I found myself joining a WhatsApp group, a founders community. The whole conversation, 24/7, was about raising money, raising money, raising money— stories about who met who, who did what, and who had gotten this much for the seed round or that round. I was like, "Okay, okay, cool."

It turns out—and this is the funniest thing—that everybody wants to give you money when you're raising capital. That's what it seems. My friend, my angel investor partner who was with me on this, started making a lot of contacts in some circles, pulling in leads.

And so, we went to see a guy who worked in gold, and we met him. We were so excited because it was actually like our first official pitch meeting. My friend had already given him the preliminaries of the idea. I was super excited. Pitching is my game. I thought, "I got this. Let's go." So, we pitched. He was super friendly and said, "This idea is amazing. My business is a family business; it's been handed down to me, so I understand small business. I'm all about small businesses. And you know what? I'll give you all the money, all of it. You have it." We were like, "What?" In my head, I was thinking, "This can't be real."

He was super serious. He asked a few questions—not many, but a few—around the numbers. My friend was amazing at handling that. We had answers for everything. He was definitely excited. He said, "Wow, you guys have got it all covered. I'm confident because you'll cover marketing, and that seems to be your thing." He was very confident with my friend, saying, "I'm going to give you the money. This is amazing. I'd love to be a part of this."

We were just stunned. We walked out, got in the car, and we were like, "Did that just happen? For real?"

Now, in life, I don't get excited about things until they really happen. So, I was excited, but I thought, "Okay, until he signs papers, I'm not fully excited." Still, I felt like, "This wasn't so difficult." At the same time, I was believing so much in my idea that I wasn't shocked. I thought, "Yeah, this is a brilliant idea. Of course, you're going to want to invest." It wasn't groundbreaking; it was like, "Yeah, that's right. That's what you should be doing—investing in this."

A couple of weeks went by. We sent him papers, we sent him everything. If I remember correctly, we offered him a really sweet deal. We weren't greedy about the percentage share we gave him. Then, he gets on the phone and says, "You know what? You're being greedy." I remember my friend handling that conversation, saying, "We're not being greedy, but we have to protect Alex, and she still needs to have at least 55% of the shares, so we can't give you all of it. You're already going to have a lot."

We even negotiated that he wouldn't give us all of the money, so it was a fair negotiation. We adjusted the amount he would contribute based on the shares he was going to get. But he literally just said, "No, you guys are greedy," and hung up the phone. I was like, "What the heck?" That was my first taste of dealing with these so-called investor people, and I thought, "Wow. Okay."

Then, we went into another meeting with another guy who came through one of my friend's contacts. This time, he was young and seemed to come from a wealthy family. It appeared he spent a lot of money and invested in early startups. That was all the background I had on this guy. The meeting was set up at a really nice, chilled, quiet restaurant during the day.

It was an informal but fine setting. I was okay with it. I took my laptop, met my friend there, and we were ready. Half an hour passed, and the guy still hadn't shown up. We were texting him, and my friend said, "He's late." I was like, "Yeah, no kidding. He's 30 minutes late." But you have to wait because you're asking for a lot of money. So, we waited. By this point, an hour and 15 minutes had passed.

I felt this was a bit of an abuse, like he was taking advantage of us wanting and needing him. It felt disrespectful. So, I wasn't the happiest. If I'm going to wait an hour and a half for you, I expect the meeting to be worth it.

Then, the guy showed up, and I honestly believe he was drunk. Or at least super hungover from a party the night before. He hugged my friend and started talking to him, completely ignoring me. It was so awkward. My friend had to introduce me, saying, "This is Alex, who I told you about."

In my head, I was thinking, "I was so close to getting up and walking out, but okay, let's entertain this." Then, he says, "Oh, I told Anna she could come," and I saw my friend's face get weirded out. I didn't know who Anna was.

Within minutes, Anna arrived, and as soon as she did, he started pampering her, moving seats around so she could sit in front of him. At this point two hours had passed, I sat there thinking, "What is going on? Are we old friends have I missed something?" I interrupted, saying, "Sorry, and who is this?"

He looked at me and said, "This is Anna." I asked, "Why is Anna joining our meeting?"

I'll never forget his face; he looked lost. My friend had to remind him, "You know, we're here to pitch the idea I told you about."

At that point, I was looking at my friend like, "What is going on? This is not okay."

My friend, tactfully, suggested swapping seats so the guy could sit next to me, and I could take him through the presentation. The guy agreed, and Anna moved. But he wasn't really paying attention; he was slouched, fidgeting, and struggling to focus. I rushed through the pitch, knowing I didn't have his attention.

During the pitch, Anna started talking to my friend about a party from the previous night. I turned around and said, "If you want to talk about your party, it's best you move tables because I'm trying to pitch here, and it would be great if there could be some respect." I was also annoyed at my friend for not stepping up. I thought, "Why did I have to do that?"

So, yeah, there were a lot of really weird stories about meeting investors who say they want to give you money.

It really seems everybody seems to love to tell you they want to give you money. It seems like an ego thing, especially after this whole experience, I've come to learn. This was mostly with men. Now, don't get me wrong, I'm not hating on all men, but this was the trend. It was an ego thing, where it made them feel powerful to say, "I'm going to give you money," like a power position. But then, nothing would come of it.

It turns out, there was another guy I met through a recommendation. This guy was very different. The meetings were amazing; he was thoughtful, thorough, and asked lots of questions. According to his background, he certainly had money, and it seemed like he was serious. This guy was solid, and we thought, "Wow, this is so cool." Even his demeanor—he was very calm, we met a couple of times, and he asked tons of questions. It felt like, "Wow, this is what it should probably be like."

So, it came to the point of signing the contract with him, this is the early contract that seals the investment agreed and shares and all the nitty gritty

And guess what? This guy just ghosts me. He completely disappears on us—on me, mainly, because I was his main point of contact. We even had a WhatsApp group, and yet he just ghosted us. Right when the time came to sign the papers after all the talk and promises—total silence. No phone calls, no WhatsApp messages.

The funniest thing is that about six to eight months later, I bumped into him at a bar I frequent. I made sure to go up to him, and his face could have turned white if that was possible. He was so embarrassed. I walked up to him, smiled, and said, "How are you?"

Eddie just stood there, staring at me like, "What?" I said, "I hope you're good." He was so perplexed. I don't even think words came out of his mouth. He just stood there, super awkward, and finally muttered, "Yeah, yeah, I'm good. And you?" I said, "Yeah," and I think he mumbled something about having some family issues. I just smiled and walked away.

Since then, I've bumped into him quite a few times, and he's always just so awkward around me. So, yeah, again everyone wants to give you money must really be a ego boost. And everyone wants to say they've got money, but when the time comes to really put the pen to paper and sign your contracts, that's when you find out who's serious.

By this point, I was running out of... I didn't know where to go next. I kept asking myself, "Where do I go to find these investors? Who do I reach out to?" I remember feeling very conflicted about how much to publicly put out there. I have such a big network—how much should I reveal about the fact that I am looking to raise money and starting a new business? Should I hide it? Because, honestly, at this point, it felt like I was hiding it. Not hiding it, but I was keeping it quiet. I wasn't talking about it, posting about it, or reaching out to my network.

I remember watching a clip from Gary V, where he said if you're looking to raise money, you have to talk to your network. You have to put it out there. That was new to me too, because for some reason, I had this hesitation about putting it out there so publicly. But then, I decided, "No, I'm going to take the leap and put it out there." I have so many people in my network, and you know how these things go—someone knows someone who knows someone.

I started pulling up my WhatsApp, going through my contacts, and drafting messages. For some, I sent voice notes. The message itself took a long time to draft because I wasn't sure what to say, how much to say. It couldn't be too long, because people don't have time for lengthy messages, but it needed to be interesting enough to catch their attention, with a hook that would make them bite, and either they'd know someone or be interested themselves.

And to be honest, it was very liberating. I'm so glad I did that. If you're going through this process and feeling similar to how I was, it's really important to start putting it out there to your network. Because at the end of the day, you actually have nothing to lose. You're trying to do something, reaching out, and you just don't know who out there is willing to help you, support you, or wants to be a part of it. Ultimately, you might connect with someone who is ready to give you the capital and money you need.

From this exercise, a lot of interesting things happened. A lot of people recommended others who had raised money for their businesses and were willing to talk to me, answer my questions, and offer advice. I was thankful for those who took the time to speak with me. I realized that there are a lot of amazing entrepreneurs out there who have raised money and are willing to help others. I got to hear interesting stories, understand what tools I needed, and checked off everything on my list.

Those conversations made me feel less alone. At this point, I didn't have anyone around me in my circle doing this, so it felt very, very lonely. The talks were great. Some people knew investors, and I followed through on a few recommendations.

HOW TO PREPARE FOR INVESTORS:

- Do your homework on them, learn as much as you can about their whole business background
- Find out what investments they have done
- Ask around from people, there's some nasty people out there and other fellow entrepreneurs might give you a heads up or the opposite!
- Prep and rehearse your pitch that you don't need to read any slides
- Come up with the toughest questions and have your colleague drill you again and again
- You need to go in feeling so ready for all the possible questions
- The moment an investor see's that you haven't thought about ever single important part and you don't have a solid answer you are loosing them

Some investors are mean and get a kick out of making it hard, you need to be ready. But you also need to be ready to know when to walk away. If they are getting disrespectful, to the point is making you feel unconfutable you WALK AWAY.

Imagine you taking money from someone who is like this? No you won't want to do that!

Yes you may need money for your idea but that does not mean you accept being treat with no respect. Don't get this ever confused!

Don't feel intimidated, or that you are less, remember potentially investing in your idea can be highly beneficial for them too so you giving them an incredible opportunity.

- **Go confident, but not cocky!**
- **Show your passion don't dim that down!**
- **Be ready for the hardest questions!**
- **Dress to impress! Smile when you are presenting, think of it as if you are telling the most interesting story!**
- **If pitching is new to you, you need to pitch as much as possible so you practice. And no this I not pitching at home, this is pitching is front of people.**

One thing I found is that there are so many groups out here for entrepreneurs raising capital, with frequent weekly meet ups and pitch nights. I joined one in Dubai and went to a couple and it was an experience!

Perfect if you want to be around the infinite talks around investing. Great to be part of a community who are doing the same as you! The people I meet were supwer supportive and warm. I only have good things to say to be honest.

It just didn't really thrill me. I want to be doing it. I don't want to be waiting hoping for that person to 'allow' me to do it. But this is me and how I want to live my life.

SOME OF THE BEST RESOURCES FOR YOU TO LEARN ABOUT RASING CAPITAL THAT I USED AND TOTALLY RECOMMEND

Y COMBINATOR YOU TUBE CHANEL

Videos to help you build a successful startup.

SLIDEBEAN YOU TUBE CHANEL

Slidebean is a venture-backed company that helps other startups navigate the complicated road to success

After all my research and learning the final best advice was combined with a lawyer, they will be able to guide to what also works best in your country. US can be very different from the UAE and so on.
So after you learn seek the advice of a lawyer who specializes in start up's

EVEN IN THE DARK THERE'S LIGHT

Where was I in all of this, and where was House of Social? Maybe you're wondering. Because this was almost a full-time job from January when I started this mission. Remember the beginning of this chapter? I had to realize that if this was going to happen, I needed to dedicate an incredible amount of time to it.

So, very early in the year, something started to happen to me, something really messed up. I was so wired to wake up and work on House of Social and my clients. Now, I was waking up and facing two tracks: House of Social and client work, or raising funds. Because if I wasn't building a brand for House of Social, creating content, new products, services, or thinking about new events, I wasn't staying relevant. The competition was getting high, and my brain started to feel so overwhelmed.

I hadn't felt this kind of overwhelm in a very long time, like years. I remember waking up, not understanding which track to follow. If I didn't focus on House of Social, how was I going to have money? Because, small detail, nobody was funding this venture—I still had to work, pay bills, and manage my life while trying to raise capital and lift this idea off the ground. The quicker I could raise money, the quicker we could start, and this could take off.

For me, it was like, "I really need to dedicate so much time to this, so we can get the investors we need and start raising capital." My brain was so overwhelmed. It was like being an athlete trained for a specific regime, and suddenly, you get thrown into a completely different situation.

I felt so out of place, confused. "How do I squeeze time for House of Social?" I kept asking myself. It was really tough, the emotional split between where to spend my time: building House of Social or raising capital and looking for money.

From January through May, that was the hardest part. I couldn't split myself into two. I'm not someone who can order 24 hours in a day, and I need headspace. We're talking about such distinct things: House of Social, which I love and is my business, versus going out to raise money, looking for investors, and being around those circles. It was really, really tough.

I'll say this was one of the biggest struggles I felt at the time. I couldn't just switch off House of Social completely. So, House of

Social ran organically for almost a year. By that, I mean I wasn't dedicating my full time to it. I wasn't packaging new programs, classes, or meetups. I completely neglected the Rebel Academy. I had clients, thank God. I did get some new clients.

And this is such a testament to the business because, even though it was running organically, I never went into a negative financial place. But I was walking on very thin ice. I had a super small salary, just getting by, and living off my savings. I told myself, "It's okay because I'm doing this for the bigger picture. The savings are there to help." But it was still really, really hard.

Two amazing new things for HOS come out of this year. My new YACHTCLASS event and the newly relaunched Rebel Club 2.0, more on this later.

But looking back, I didn't see it at the time, but these two thing crucial. The first was my yacht class event. I don't even know how I managed to pull it off like that.

I think it was something inside me saying, "I need to do something for House of Social. I can't just be inactive." The Yachtclass was an idea and concept I had for years, even before COVID. It was something I'd been holding on to and find the best timing. Well the timing had arrived!

The idea was to combine mini-classes, networking, and business showcases, all on a yacht. It super fun. I gave it a 1950's sailor vibe very Christina Aguilera Candymen video vibes!

I launched the event and it got sold out in a week! It was the most fun, the most enjoyable event I'd done in ages. It felt like I was starving for not doing anything for House of Social.

That event also marked a new era for me, understanding that I didn't want to do events the same way anymore. I wanted to shift more into entertainment. People loved the idea of being on a yacht, learning, networking, and showcasing their brands. That was the beginning of my realization: I was done with the same concepts everyone was doing.

So, it was such a happy place. It was such a win. I needed that for me. I needed that event more than anyone else who came and bought tickets, and I'm so grateful to them, but it was almost like I needed to do it for me. It reminded me of the entrepreneur I am, the creator I am, the creative person I can be because this whole process of raising capital was starting to feel very defeating.

CHAPTER 10

When To Walk Away

I was starting to come to some realizations. At this point, if we're looking at the timeline correctly, I had already been working on this for a year. Raising money was almost a 9 to 12-month process at this point, even starting the year before in the last quarter.

And then, I realized something. I was miserable.

What do I mean by that? I didn't want to wake up. That's big for me because I love waking up. I love the day; I love what I do. But I didn't want to wake up anymore. I was so incredibly miserable. I was sad, and I had lost my confidence as an entrepreneur—something I had felt so strongly for a very long time. Not like this. Sure, there are days you might lose your confidence, but those are just days. This time, I had lost my confidence for weeks, for months.

I was sad. I was in a really bad financial place. I hardly had any money. I wasn't going out, not that I even spend a lot, but my life in Dubai is quite simple. Yet, anything I did, I was worrying about money. And that is never a good place when you're not financially secure.

I wasn't feeling good. I was feeling quite miserable and defeated. When summer arrived, I left. I went to Portugal, barely having the money to buy my ticket. I just wanted to get out of Dubai.

During this time, there was this one investor, someone I had reached out to when I began reaching out to anyone in my contacts who could be a potential lead. Initially, he didn't reply—nothing. I think I did a second or third follow-up, still nothing. This would have been maybe in January or February. Then, a few months later, I woke up one day and thought, "I'm going to call him again. I'm just going to try." So I did, and this time he actually replied. He said he was interested.

Now, this contact came through some people who work with him, and he's definitely a high-net-worth individual. We have close mutual connections, and I had met him a few years ago. On WhatsApp, his replies were short. He asked for the pitch deck, and I sent it. He replied with a "Sure." Always very short. Then he asked for a smaller, condensed version. Smaller than the 10-slide deck.

Over the next few weeks, he asked a couple of questions, which we answered. He asked, "Is this how much you need?" We replied to his questions about the finances, and he said, "I'm interested." This took about two to three months to get to that point. Your level of patience with this process needs to be huge because it takes time. We were a bit in shock because, for the first time in a while, this felt credible.

I asked, "Do you want to Zoom? We should all Zoom." But he was like, "No need to Zoom. We can manage." We thought, okay, people with a lot of money are busy, that's fine. We exchanged a few emails with questions, and he wanted a lot of the equity shares. I remember being at a bar when he emailed me—he's not in the UAE, he travels a lot, so the time zones could be anything.

He had asked for quite a big stake in exchange for giving us the whole amount we were looking for. I remember my friend calling me, saying, "Alex, you have to make the final decision. Are you okay with him having that many shares?" I was always protected—I still had the majority. But it meant we would have an investor with a significant share. I made the decision, "Yeah, let's do it. Let's give it to him. He's going to fund us, and we'll launch. Let's go."

He agreed, and I thought, "Wow, maybe there is a light at the end of all this." Because even though I was feeling really bad and not okay, I never stopped believing. I just never did. I never doubted it, never wanted to quit. I'm very determined that way. But I was feeling it; I wasn't in a good place.

So, summer comes, and this investor says, "I'm traveling during the summer, getting married, going on my honeymoon. After summer, we'll get the papers done, and everything will be signed."

That summer was filled with anguish. "Is it going to happen? It has to happen." But I found myself with my whole life hanging by a thread, dependent on one person. You compensate by telling yourself, "Well, it's because of my idea, and it's a great idea, so it makes up for it." But as the days, weeks, and months passed, that concept I was telling myself began to corrode.

By the end of summer, I knew it. I remember looking at my mom and realizing how insanely miserable I was. I said, "If he doesn't come through, I'm going to walk away from this."

Let's remember why I began all of this. Why did I take that leap? I took it because I wanted to be happy. As hard as entrepreneurship is, I need to be happy. This was not making me happy, and I had given it a lot of time. It was almost a year and a half at this point since day one, and I felt miserable. I didn't want to get out of bed. I had no money. House of Social, which is my livelihood, was neglected because I had to give time to this. I was sad. I didn't want to get up. I had no joy. I had lost myself, and my future was hanging on a decision from one guy.

I remember having this "wake-up" moment, like, "Whoa, no. My whole future, my entire life, financially, everything—from the financial aspect to the idea, to what I'm going to build—you're telling me it's all on this guy's shoulders?"

No. Hell no. No. It was like, "No, I don't think this is for me." That was the end of August, beginning of September. That was the beginning of me realizing that maybe this wasn't for me, and I didn't want to do it anymore. It had nothing to do with the idea.

So, I was very clear on what was happening. If he pulled through, okay. But remember, it had been a year and a half of me believing, spending the whole summer hoping things would change, hoping everything would be okay. But that was just what I was telling myself, because deep down, I didn't feel okay.

I returned to Dubai and began reaching out again, saying, "Hey, it's now September. I hope you had a great summer." We started talking to our lawyers to get the contract terms drafted. Once you agree verbally with an investor, you need a contract that solidifies the agreement. The signing of this contract is what makes it real, with all the clauses outlined.

We were very excited. I spoke to a few lawyers, found a great one, and she helped draft the contract. That was a new experience for me. I remember being so excited, thinking, "This is like what I see in movies!" Clause after clause, and you need so much patience to go through it all. We sent it to him, and he replied, "Okay, yes, the contract seems fine."

But he didn't sign. He just went quiet for three to four weeks, and this was another aggravating part of raising capital—things take time. You're not going to get an immediate reply. Weeks can pass before you hear anything.

He disappeared for three weeks, no reply, and I was left thinking he was probably just really busy. He owned a couple of companies, traveled a lot.

Then, one night, I got an email from him: "Sorry, I just don't think this is the right fit for me."

Boom! I don't know what I was more upset about—the fact that we had come so far with him, or that he was so full of "yeses," to the point where we even got a lawyer to draft the contract. Everything seemed like it was a go, and then it wasn't.

I felt angry and frustrated, like I'd been dragged along. On the other hand, there was also a sense of relief. I reverted back to my spirituality, looking for signs. I had missed the signs along this journey. It's important to have a healthy balance between determination and knowing when to stop. You need to stay the course, but if everything around you is negative, you have to weigh it and decide. By the end of it, it all added up: I was miserable, and everything was a roadblock.

And thankfully, by the end of 2023, I made the decision. In October or November, I officially closed that chapter and walked away. I put it in a box, and it was such a relief.

That's why 2024 is the comeback year. If you didn't know the story, you wouldn't have seen anything on the outside. 2024 has been a special year for me. It's been the year of coming back. We are almost at the end of the year, and I can tell you it's been one of the most financially strong years we've had in nine years.

I needed to get a bit derailed. I needed to go rogue in a new direction, and that brought a new perspective.

The point is, don't think your path as an entrepreneur will be linear. Don't be afraid to go left or right, try different paths, and take risks. You might just find your way back or discover something new. **The best thing that happened was trying something new. It did something to me. It re-energized me.**

Ultimately, there are no regrets. I don't go to bed thinking, "What if?" I am at peace, and that is all that matters.

I learned about raising capital, how to attract investors, how to value a company, and, most importantly, that people love to tell you they want to give you money, and it's often just a bunch of empty promises.

Why it always pays off to try is because you always get answers, you get so much clarity.

A lot of people only want to try with a guarantee that is going to work out, so they will find all the reasons and excuses to delay doing it.

Perfectionism is insecurity disguised, so stop celebrating and making it your excuse.

You should be really happy and confident that you are going to give it a shoot! You are going to give it your absolute best and that in itself in a world where most people are judging and pointing fingers is already a win.

You are going to love the journey and the process and learn so much and that will make you a better human, marketer and entrepreneur.

To say that you had the courage to try is everything! Versus dying with regrets. Regret is poison.

Don't live a life with regrets! With 'what if's'. Instead live a life filled with incredible stories that you can cherish, laugh about and share and that gifted with you growth!

CHAPTER 11

The Come Back Kid

This is the first time I'm sharing this story in such an open, vulnerable way, and I wish I had shared this with you back when it was happening. It all happened earlier this year, so it's still quite recent, even though it feels like ages ago. I kicked off 2024 really laser-focused. If you've read the previous chapter, you'll know this was my comeback year. After a challenging year and a half, 2024 was all about bouncing back — a fresh start.

You know how it is; like an athlete, you get used to a certain discipline. As an entrepreneur, you become super disciplined with your schedule, your mindset, your ideas, and your strategies. But when that routine changes, it throws you off. You have to find your rhythm again, and that was my mission this year. I had put the past behind me, walked away from that chapter, and refocused on my first baby, House of Social — the most important part of my career. I began the year with a plan, determined to execute it flawlessly. Nothing was going to stop me.

So there I was, in January, launching a big campaign for my Rebel Club. The Rebel Club came out of a year that felt a bit weird — a year when I was trying to launch my second business. But that's the thing about new ventures; even if things don't go exactly as planned, there's always room for a little magic. During that year, while I was trying so hard to get my new business off the ground, I gave myself permission to create something new for House of Social. I set out to create at least one or two new products or offerings. And that's when I decided to bring back the Rebel Club.

Now, the first edition of Rebel Club didn't exactly take off. And that's okay! Here's a little reminder: sometimes, when you launch something new, it doesn't work out the first time around. More often than not, it doesn't. Sure, it's awesome when it does, but most of the time, you need to tweak and try again.

The Rebel Club was something I launched a few years ago, offering a super affordable monthly fee — just 100 dirhams — for access to free live classes with Alex. People signed up in droves. Honestly, it was probably the easiest money I ever made. But here's the thing: out of 60 or 70 people who signed up, only 4 or 5 showed up to the live classes. I felt miserable. This wasn't what I wanted. I was taking people's money, but they weren't getting value out of it. It led to a big argument with my mom (a.k.a. my CFO). She was like, "This is easy money!" And I was like, "Yeah, but my ethos, purpose, and legacy matter more."

For me, the number one priority for House of Social, and everything I do, is whether it's bringing value to people. Is it making an impact? This wasn't. People weren't showing up to the classes, and yes, they were paying, but I didn't want to just take their money. So, I knew I had to close it. I wrote an email to everyone who was subscribed, saying, "Listen, I'm closing this because it's not working. Many of you are paying but not showing up, and I'm not here to just take your money. I want to create products and services that make a real impact, and we're not there yet." And so, I closed the Rebel Club.

But deep down, I always knew there was something there — something special about the idea of a membership where people could pay a monthly fee for consistent support. After nine years of consultancy, I've learned that the key to achieving results is consistency. Call it coaching, consultancy, support, or guidance — it's that regular, ongoing connection that makes a difference.

So, I realized there was a way to make Rebel Club work. I decided to create a budget-friendly option where members could spend one hour with me each month for $107 (395 dirhams). It would be a one-on-one membership, unlike the typical group sessions that are everywhere (and that I can offer for free). The new Rebel Club now has three membership tiers, which is super exciting! And guess what? This time, it worked!

This is a little testament to all of you reading: **if you have an idea that failed but you feel in your gut there's something there, don't give up. Give it time and keep reworking it.**

CEASE & DESIST...?! SAY WHAT

In January 2024, I was in full swing, launching the second enrolment phase for the Rebel Club. I was all in — sending emails, promoting it left and right — when I got a message on LinkedIn. It was from a guy we'll call Johnny, and it was not a nice message. Johnny claimed I was stealing his trademark. He said, "I have a Rebel Club. You're using my trademark. I have a Marketing Rebel Club."

Now, here's the twist: my Rebel Club has always been "Alex's Rebel Club." But whenever I relaunch something or start a new campaign, I like to refresh things. It just so happened that this time, I added the word "Marketing" to Rebel Club, calling it "Alex's Marketing Rebel Club."

Looking back, I can laugh at how many things felt glitchy. It was like the universe was sending me hints. Back in December and January, I wasn't feeling my usual burst of creative inspiration for the campaign. It felt weird. I even remember thinking, "Why is there this odd energy blocking me?" I brushed it off, thinking maybe I was just tired.

But I pushed through, made the videos, and in them, I'm a spacewoman (because, why not?) taking you and your business to new heights. I needed to have fun with it. Yet, looking back, I wasn't happy with the videos. I forced myself to do them, took the pictures, created the campaign, and knew something wasn't quite right.

Anyway, I launched it as "Alex's Marketing Rebel Club," and then came Johnny's message. I don't know about you, but when I get long LinkedIn messages, I tend to skim through them. Johnny's started off brutal: "You call yourself a professional? You're stealing my Marketing Rebel Club." He continued, "This is the first warning. You need to take everything down, or I'll take legal action." He even mentioned other experts and threw in a long copyright lesson.

My reaction? "Who is this guy?" I ignored it and continued with my campaign. A week later, another message from Johnny — same story. Again, I ignored it.

Then, I was sending out weekly mailers for the Rebel Club when I got an email reply. It was Johnny again, but this time he was nastier. I thought, "Okay, now he's in my inbox." But honestly, I didn't have time for this. I'm used to hate and bullying, so I didn't let it consume me. I skimmed through it and moved on.

Then, about two weeks later, I woke up one morning around 6 a.m. to an email titled "Cease and Desist." I didn't know much about legal stuff, but I'd seen enough movies to know this wasn't good. It felt like seeing an expiry date and thinking, "Maybe I should pay attention to this." I opened the email, and it wasn't from Johnny — he was just CC'd. It was from his lawyer.

The email was an official cease and desist, claiming I had breached Johnny's trademark for the "Marketing Rebel Club," and they were threatening legal action. They said they would file complaints on all the online platforms I was using.

Just to clarify: I'm in Dubai, UAE, and Johnny is in the U.S. So, his lawyer was essentially trying to take legal action against someone in a different country over a trademark. That's when I thought, "Okay, maybe I need to give this some attention."

But I wasn't scared or freaking out. I thought, "What's the next step? How do we fix this?" I realized I'd have to dedicate some time to this issue, which was annoying because I was in the middle of planning my Yacht Class event.

The Yacht Class event is one of my favorites. It's all about storytelling through fun, creative videos, and I was super excited about it. But now, I had to make room for this trademark issue. So, I talked to a good friend — shoutout to her, you know who you are — who's a lawyer in the U.S., which was super helpful. I showed her the LinkedIn messages and the cease and desist, and we discussed my options.

And here's where I learned a lot about trademarks. Lesson number one: trademarks are valid per country. You don't just buy a trademark, and it's global. His trademark was valid in the U.S., but not in the UAE. So, we established that.

But this is where things got murky. Johnny's biggest threat was filing complaints on all the online platforms I used, saying, "You're posting on LinkedIn, and LinkedIn is American-owned, so my trademark is valid there." He went on about how hard he worked to get his Marketing Rebel Club to rank on Google, claiming I was trying to take that from him.

I mean, seriously, how could anyone confuse us? I'm a spacewoman, and he's a white, fat American guy. There's no way people were mixing us up! I felt sad thinking, "Can't we just all be rebels together?" From the start, it was an attack, and that's what upset me.

Talking to my lawyer, we realized the options: tell Johnny to get lost and keep using "Marketing Rebel Club," or take out the word "marketing." But the problem was, we didn't know how platforms like Meta, GoDaddy, or LinkedIn would handle an American trademark complaint. It was out of our hands.

So, I thought, "If one word is what's stopping my success, I'll take the word 'marketing' out." I didn't need it. I could still make Rebel Club work. In less than 30 minutes, I went to my website, changed the banner, and removed "Marketing." It was back to "Alex's Rebel Club," and that was that.

After that, I realized, "I need to figure out this whole trademarking thing." I'd never really thought about it before because I still felt like a little Nemo, a small fish in a big sea. I thought, "Why do I need a trademark?" And when launching a business in the UAE, where everything is already so expensive, why add another expense? Trademarking always seemed a bit fancy to me, and I never thought I needed it.

But after this, it became clear I needed to protect my business. So, I talked to my official lawyer, and we started the process of trademarking House of Social in the UAE, which can cost around 13,000 to 15,000 dirhams.

We started the process of trademarking House of Social, and I needed to move fast. Trademarking in the UAE costs around 13,000 to 15,000 dirhams because you can't do it yourself. You need a power of attorney, and they handle it for you. I'll tell you more about this later because I went on to trademark in Portugal too. In Portugal, you can do it yourself through an easy online portal, and it's much more cost-friendly. So, at this point, the goal was to protect House of Social. Suddenly, it was early February, and I had to pull out around 13,000 to 15,000 dirhams from my cash flow to get it done. Thankfully, I had the funds ready, so that was one less thing to worry about.

And then, what happens next?

One morning, I woke up, got ready to send out an email alert, and was in the middle of my Yacht Class event, trying to sell tickets. If you've ever promoted an event, you know how much work it takes — creating content, sending direct messages, and emailing everyone. I opened my laptop, logged into my Mailchimp account, and there was a big red strip saying, "Your account has been temporarily deactivated." My heart sank. I saw an email from Mailchimp saying they'd received a trademark complaint, and I had 48 hours to fix it.

Let me tell you, that was the moment it all became real. I thought, "Wow, this is serious." I'd been using Mailchimp for nine years, and suddenly, my account was deactivated. That's when I truly got scared. I started thinking, "What's next? Will I lose my Instagram?

My Facebook? My LinkedIn? What about GoDaddy, where my domain is?" I was freaking out.

The thing is, by the time I got the email from Mailchimp, I replied within 48 hours (actually much less) and said, "Here's my website, proving there's no trademark violation." I even went ahead and removed some videos that had "Marketing Rebel Club" in them. Funny enough, there weren't many, so it wasn't a lot of work, but I remember doing it and just crying, thinking, "How is it that some guy in the U.S. has this much control over my content?" That was not a happy moment for me. I even filmed myself crying, saying, "I can't believe this is happening. I can't believe someone in the U.S. has this kind of power."

But I kept telling myself, "Just do it. Pick your battles, and move forward." So I wrote back to Mailchimp, showing them there was no trademark infringement. I even sent them links to my Instagram and Facebook to show I'd complied. I thought, "That's it, it should be resolved."

You won't believe it, but it took three weeks for Mailchimp to respond. Three weeks where I couldn't use my account. Sure, I had my data backed up, but it wasn't neatly segmented or tagged. So, I had to quickly switch to another email provider — I chose Wix. It ended up being the best decision, but that's another story.

So, here I was, trying to promote my event and sell tickets, and I had to carve out four hours of my day to shift everything to a new email platform. And yes, I know how to do this stuff, but it still created stress and chaos during an already hectic time. Three weeks later, Mailchimp finally responded with a two-line email saying, "We cannot reopen your account because you still have email campaigns mentioning 'Alex's Marketing Rebel Club.' As long as these campaigns are on our platform, it's a trademark violation."

And I thought, "You've taken three weeks to tell me this?" By then, I was beyond done with Mailchimp. I wrote back, "I've deleted everything. You can check. Why did it take three weeks to tell me this? Clearly, you don't care about your customers." I tried reaching their customer service chat, their helpline, their legal email — nothing.

About a month later, they finally replied, saying, "We will get back to you. We're reviewing your account." By that point, I was done. I had moved on to Wix, and I wasn't looking back.

This was when I truly felt things could get serious. That's when I started to get scared. I went into full protection mode, moving my domain from GoDaddy to Wix so they couldn't mess with it. I was just trying to make sure my bases were covered. Unfortunately, there wasn't much I could do about Meta or LinkedIn, so I had to hope for the best there. But at least I felt somewhat protected.

We filed for the trademark process in two categories: consulting and education, under House of Social. It was scary because I had no control, and I'd never been in this kind of situation before.

Johnny then sent another email, which was very threatening and mean. I told my lawyer, "I don't want to engage with him anymore. You handle it." My lawyer replied to Johnny, telling him to stop threatening me. She said I had shown goodwill by removing "marketing" and taking down some posts. She made it clear that it was time to move on.

Johnny sent yet another long, threatening email, but we didn't respond. We were done.

During this time, I felt really scared and anxious. I remember having to sign the power of attorney papers for the trademark process, and I felt so overwhelmed. I'm not great with paperwork, and I was just so scared. I even had to give a keynote at a conference the morning my Mailchimp account was deactivated. I didn't want to go. I felt like my whole world was being shaken.

One of my friends came over to join me at the conference, and when she saw me, she said, "Alex, you don't look good." I hadn't even washed my face, and I looked like I'd been hit by a truck. But my grandmother always taught me, "The show must go on." So, I thought, "I'm not going to let this guy have this much power over me. I'm going to show up." I got ready quickly, went to the conference, and it ended up being great. I was proud of myself for not letting this mess stop me.

My mom always said, "When everything is falling apart, hold on tight and keep moving forward, even if it's just a tiny step." February was a really hard month.

The YachtClass event was a whole other drama. There were endless issues with the boat and the logistics. And, to top it all off, there were massive thunderstorms in Dubai, so we had to cancel the event on Saturday morning. Luckily, we moved it to the next day, but by then, I felt like I'd been hit by a baseball bat over and over again.

Trademarking in Dubai is a long process. It takes about six months, and even after approval, there's a public period where people can contest it. So you're never fully safe, but I just wanted to get through it and move on.

PROTECT YOUR BRAND

I learned so many lessons from this. You never know when someone like Johnny might come after you. So, consider trademarking your business, even if you're a small fish in the big sea. Trademarking helps protect you. Start by registering in the country where you operate and then expand as your business grows.

I shared this story with my YachtClass attendees, and it felt so good to get it out. While this was happening, I wanted so badly to share it on Instagram because communicating is one of my love languages. But I had to stay quiet, and that was really hard for me.

Sharing is therapeutic for me. It helps me, and it can help others. But I had to keep showing up for my content, for my presence online, and for my events, even though this was happening behind the scenes. Only my mom, my lawyer friend, and a few close friends knew what was going on.

This is the first time I'm sharing this story publicly. It was a really scary time because my business is a big part of my self-worth. To suddenly wake up and realize that everything could be taken away from you, that your name and your business could just disappear — it's terrifying.

This experience triggered a lot of old trauma. My father abandoned me and hurt me emotionally, and this situation brought up those feelings again. It was like, "How is it that another man is having this impact on me?" It was very triggering.

I wouldn't wish this experience on anyone. If you haven't trademarked your business yet, seriously consider it. If you're in the UAE, talk to a good lawyer. Remember, you might need to trademark in different categories, like education or consultancy, depending on your business. It can be expensive, but it's worth it.

This story is a reminder to never let anyone take away your joy or spirit. No matter how horrible their actions might be, don't let them have that power over you. When I look back at that tough month of February, I'm proud of myself for showing up every day, even if it was just at 5% or 20%. That's still amazing.

Some days, I wanted to hide, and that's okay too. I took moments for myself to hide and recover, but I kept moving forward. Surround yourself with good people who can support you, listen to you, and remind you that you've got this.

Get good legal advice, learn the law, and know that you can stand strong and protect your business. Keep taking steps forward, even if they're small. After all 2024 is the come back year!

CHAPTER 12

The Pursuit of Happiness

Dear Rebel, as you're reading this, it could be 2024, 2025, or any time in the future. I want to remind you that by sharing my journey, my experiences, my ups, and my downs, my hope is to make you feel less alone and infuse you with confidence and courage that YES if you CHOOSE to get comfortable with the unconfortable. If you make a solid practical decision to choose to believe in yourself. There is absolutely no stopping you in this life!

I want to show you that the snippets we see on social media, those small, perfect-looking snapshots, often don't tell the full story. They can make it seem like everyone else has it all figured out, that they've got their lives perfectly together. But life isn't linear. Your path won't always be straight and clear. It's wonderful when things align, and there are seasons in our lives where everything feels like it's falling perfectly into place. But the real beauty of life is in its twists and turns—the bumps, the highs, the lows, the moments of stillness, confusion, and pure joy. If you don't give yourself the courage to take leaps, to be curious, to explore new places, ideas, projects, or even countries, how will you truly experience all that life has to offer?

We are so lucky to be alive and to have this chance to live. Find the courage to say yes, to take risks, and give yourself the opportunity to live some of the best adventures you might ever have. You only live once. You only get this one shot.

By sharing my life and experiences, my hope is to inspire you to be more confident, more courageous, and yes, more rebellious in making bold choices for your life. Because nobody else will make them for you.

No one is just going to hand you the courage or give you permission to chase your dreams. It has to come from within you. You need to find out what's holding you back, work on that, and heal from it so you can grow closer to the version of yourself you are meant to be. You are meant to go after everything you want. So, that idea, that project, that dream you keep putting off or finding excuses to delay—now is the time to act. We have the present, and we don't know what the future holds. The last thing you want is to be weighed down by regrets. Regret is a heavy, negative energy that can eat away at your happiness.

You don't want to sit with your friends, family, or grandchildren someday with stories of "what ifs." You want to tell stories of the "remember when!" full of courage, risk, and adventure. So, no matter the pressure from family, society, or culture—none of that matters but you. It's your life, not someone else's opinion of it. What others think of you, that's their perception, their agenda. That's not you.

When your journey ends, it's your name that will be on the tombstone, not theirs.

I am so excited to share these last chapters with you, covering the past few years of my life. I don't know if this is the end of *It's a Good Day to Be a Rebel,* or if we'll be moving on to a whole new book in the future. I hope you hold onto these chapters, revisit them when needed, and highlight the sections that speak to you. There are exercises, reminders, and checklists throughout this book that you can keep coming back to, and I hope it serves as a manual, a companion, to remind you that you are never alone.

If you've read this far I'm incredibly grateful, I would LOVE to hear from you, a hello, what chapters or parts of this book have resonated with you the most! You can what's app me on +971502455136 or Instagram DM me @alexhouseofsocial, write me an email alex@alexhouseofsocial.com. I'd love to say hi, and I can't wait to hear about what you're working on!

Thank you for reading, and remember that happiness is the goal—to be happy. For so many years on this entrepreneurial journey, I wrapped my self-worth and happiness around my career. It's incredible to have a career you're proud of, one that consumes you because of your passion for it. I've learned a new lesson recently, though—it's great to be so proud of your work, to put your heart and soul into it, but we cannot wrap all our self-worth and fulfillment around a business.

Business is volatile; it can change, disappear, or even become something you decide to walk away from. So, find the things that make you happy on a deeper level, things that fulfill you in a big way, because business or no business, those things will always stay. That is the foundation you need to stand on. This has been one of my most recent lessons—that I need to keep seeking parts of my life that fulfill and make me more happy. I love what I do so immensely but I haven't been feeling entirely happy with certain other parts of my life.

I remember when I shared something similar with Gary Vee and told him, ' well when I'm working I'm happy but the then other stuff is making me sad…" and he follows to tell me I'm micro happy I'm not in the macro HAPPY! And that now more then ever is my next adventure. I'm grateful that career wise I found what I love in a huge gigantic way but now I need to work out other parts of this rebel life!

That's my new journey now, and I'm excited to see how it unfolds in 2025. I'll surely be sharing it with you and if you read this chapter many things will follow to make sense.

So, thank you. Thank you for reading, for being here, and for taking this journey with me. I can't wait to hear from you, and I wish you the courage to live life boldly, to chase your dreams fiercely, to be DELICIOUSLY REBELIOUS to find your own path—whatever it may look like but that is yours!

With so much love and sparkle teal dust, Alex

IT'S A GOOD DAY TO BE A REBEL

FREE REBEL ACADEMY

Streaming 74+ Free classes!

On the road to a 100…

WWW.ALEXHOUSEOFSOCIAL.COM/
FREEREBELACADEMY

Created to help you navigate the world of Social & Digital Media for endless opportunities

As of writing this book in October 2024, my Rebel Academy now hosts 74 free classes and courses. That's right, 74! This is an extraordinary milestone, but I'm not stopping there. I'm on a mission to reach 100 free courses. So, if you're picking up this book in 2025, chances are there are already 100 free classes and courses streaming just for you. Go ahead, find me another platform giving you this many courses—I'll wait.

The most exciting part? The complete revamp of the Rebel Academy. I've transformed the student dashboard, and it's like nothing you've seen before. I asked myself, "How can I make the learning experience better, smoother, and more badass for my rebels?" And the answer was simple:

Turn it into a Netflix-style experience. That's right, it looks just like your favorite Netflix dashboard—the one you probably use for all your Netflix and chill sessions. But ours? It's turquoise, sleek, and designed to serve you the best of branding, sales, marketing strategies, personal branding, and more.

It's got all the different tracks neatly laid out so you can easily jump straight to what you need. The covers look stunning, and you can even resume right where you left off. It's a super smooth, user-friendly learning experience, packing a punch with all those classes and courses.

But wait, there's more! 2024 has been all about free webinar marathons. Yup, I've been hosting a series of them. As of now, I've thrown down three amazing

Free marathon webinars, delivering a total of 30 brand-new

classes!

That's right, I started with a 10-webinar free marathon, followed by a five-session sprint, and most recently, a 15-webinar marathon in September and October. The topics? Fresh and relevant—covering everything from podcasting to content creation, and even finding your confidence.

So, if it's been a while since you last checked out my free Rebel Academy, it's time for a comeback. Not enrolled yet? What are you waiting for? Keep an eye out for my next Webinar Marathons because they're free, packed with value, and come with an incredible WhatsApp group that you definitely want to be part of.

Welcome to the one and only, most amazing free Rebel Academy out there, where there's absolutely no excuse for you not to have access to all the information and skills you need. I can't wait to see you on the other side.

Enroll here and access all the free classes + my Rebel Academy Whatsapp Group!
www.alexhouseofsocial.com/freerebelacademy

IT'S A GOOD DAY TO BE A REBEL

REBEL CLUB

THE ONLY 101 CONSULTANCY CLUB MADE FOR AMBTIOUS PEOPLE!

Dress Code: Ambition!

WWW.ALEXHOUSEOFSOCIAL.COM/ REBELCLUB

I'm going to be as bold as to say that my exclusive consultancy, REBEL CLUB, is the only membership club for ambitious people. REBEL CLUB is my consultancy offering for those who want to work one-on-one with me. The most exciting aspect since launching REBEL CLUB has been the RISE TIER. This tier is a very budget-friendly option, where you can "borrow my brains" 1hr a month,101 with me, online or in person for 109$ a month at the time of writing this book. Please check the REBEL CLUB page for the latest prices.

There are three membership options: RISE, SAVAGE, and FIERCE, offering more hours for you to work with me, where I can also build and create things for you! You can upgrade or downgrade to suit your goals.

Since launching the REBEL CLUB membership, it has provided consistent support to many entrepreneurs, marketers, and rebels in between. The truth is, without consistent support, you might start to lose direction. Nothing beats the power of having ongoing guidance. I am in your corner—supporting, guiding, and giving you practical, real strategies. You have WhatsApp support, online calls, and in-person meetings. Nothing beats this ongoing support to ensure that you are always on the right track, waking up super confident.

Some people might wonder why I call it a club if it's a one-on-one consultancy. The reason is the power of community that I've created around my clients. Many of my clients have gone on to collaborate with each other on campaigns, events, and projects. We have a WhatsApp group where everyone shares what they are working on, and you will also be part of my client ecosystem. You can leverage their platforms and brands to create great collaborations.

If you're interested in working one-on-one with me, take a peek inside the Rebel Club. The dress code is ambition. There's no happy hour—ambition and hard work run 24/7 when you're working with me. I can't wait to see you on the other side!

Go to **www.alexhouseofsocial.com/rebelclub**

Whatsapp me on +971502455136 if you want to talk to me before signing up!

REBEL GUEST CHAPTERS

Breaking Free From Abuse:

The Courage to Rebel and Rise Again

By Fernanda Carvalho

The Power of Pacing Your Peaks

By Helen Farmer

Breaking Free From Abuse: The Courage to Rebel and Rise Again

By Fernanda Carvalho

When my daughter talks about It's a Good Day to be a Rebel, this made me think.

What is to be a Rebel? Dictionary says that a Rebel is "*a person who rises in opposition or armed resistance against an established government or leader.*" Our society usually sees Rebels as bad people, wrong people.

I don't agree. I've been a Rebel all my life. I was raised kind of like a princess, in a very stable environment with all the right ingredients: mum, dad, brothers, cats, dog, school, security, identity and above all, a future!

One day, all of that was taken away from me. All of it was gone because some people, somewhere made decisions I was oblivious to. No more country, friends, future and .. identity? Who was I? Where did I belong? I saw myself in a strange country and was told: this is your country and now you are Portuguese. What the f*** was that? who were those people around me? They were speaking my language but we couldn't communicate. They were ugly and mean because they saw me as a threat, a stranger that was occupying their space. And then, I got married imagining that would bring me a piece of what I had lost.

Didn't work. So, I Rebelled!

I walked away. From the country, the husband, the '*right thing to do*'. And the right thing to do was to stay at home, look after the house, the husband, learn how to cook, have a few noisy children, get fat and obey. No! I Rebelled.

Materially I had nothing. No money, no bank account, no job, my daughter was 18 months old and I was living in a country which law used to say: *the husband is the master of the house*. Without his permission, I couldn't leave with my daughter. He even used to go out with her, nice, elegant, gorgeous man and extremely rich and lock the house so I couldn't go out. Ah, but before leaving the house he would also lock the phone in a cabinet.

I think I forgot the part that he regularly abused me physically but then, locked in the house who would see or know? I could visit my parents from time to time but only '*if I behaved well*'! Prison!

And then, my father had passed away. Dad was the strong trunk, the example in my life. Our name is Carvalho, which means oak tree. That's what he was.

But then, I realized I'm Carvalho as well. So, I Rebelled.

I slammed a door in my face, went to the police, accused him of hitting me, fought for two months and won. I won the divorce and I won full guardianship of my daughter.

I had another Carvalho by my side: my mum and without her I wouldn't be able to have made my life as I made. Alex would not be who she is.

I started working at the airport at a time that woman wouldn't work in this type of operation, I have done everything and a bit more to grow up, and up, and up and I've done so because I Rebelled. Over and over and over again.

I Rebelled against prejudices, against statutes, against "*women should stay at home and not hang around in airplanes carrying loads*".

I Rebelled against the women who never supported me and against the men who tried to put me down. I was very young and it took me a while to understand why women don't support other women who grow up, but then I realized: they aren't capable of Rebelling. They stay there making the best rice in the world and putting a lace tablecloth and plastic flowers on the dining room table and always saying yes.

Every night I came home from the airport very late and my mum's brilliant intelligence always allowed me to have time with my daughter. She did everything the other way round. She Rebelled against the 'norm': she would let Alex sleep when she came home from school so that she could wake up around dinner time to play, do homework and be awake when I arrived. My mum was unique, brilliant a zillion years ahead of the world.

My family is a family of Rebels: my father was a highly respected judge who threw everything into the air to set up on his own and had the biggest and most renowned law firm in all of Angola.

My mum already dyed her hair green in the 70s, designed her own clothes and was an opera singer. Unlike other women of her time, she didn't care if I learnt to cook and embroider like other girls my age because she said: *she studies, works and then pays someone to do it!*

Many times in my life, I've had to rebel against circumstances. Like when I used so-called 'less legal' means to bring in 'goods' to survive; like when I had to take my mother and daughter and move to England; Alex doesn't have very good memories of her life in England but I'm very grateful that I made that decision. That's what allowed her to stay away from the poverty of society that this country was and the abuse of her father; like when I decided to go to Brazil to audit a company that had all sorts of crooks and I even received death threats. In short, I would have many stories to tell but this is not my place.

What I mean is that all of it, absolutely all of it, only happened because I always rebelled.

When you're a Rebel, your path is almost always lonely. People either don't understand or in most cases are simply envious.

That doesn't bother me one bit.

Look at the eagle: the eagle proudly flies high, very high and alone.

Anyone can be a Rebel. You just have to believe in it. To believe that there is always a way. To believe that we didn't come into this world to be unhappy, trampled underfoot by others.

Nobody takes anybody's place. We all have our space and we need to do the best we can with it. It's a space that passes very quickly. Being Rebellious is good, it's healthy. I'm so proud of being a Rebel!

It's not necessarily easy. No, but in life you never have everything of everything. So, choose! Choose the path that leads forward, upwards. Turn the table upside down! Rebel.

Unfortunately, many women today are still abused by their families, by society and by their husbands. I've never hidden the fact that I was abused by a man, by my husband, because I'm proud to have Rebelled.

Yes, it is possible – by finding the strength and the reason for it within ourselves. Rebel for yourself, for yourself. Raise your head up.

Don't allow yourself to think that it's not possible, that you don't have the means, that you have children and all those "*reasons*" that come to mind. That's all dust. Dust to stop you seeing clearly that there is another way.

I believe mum, and what she always heard about my dad and myself, showed Alex, all along her life, the good side of being a Rebel. Always be respectful, but choose the path that's right for her. And if she has to fly high like an eagle, she has to look for other eagles. She is a Rebel. She is a Carvalho too.

Rebel! Raise your head up because you can and it's within each one of us to decide that Today is the Best Day of Your Life to be a Rebel!

Lots of love, Mum, AKA Luke, AKA Fernanda

About Fernanda Carvalho

I am an experienced manager with a strong background in customer service, known for my strategic mindset and positive attitude in tackling challenging business situations. With expertise in problem-solving, conflict resolution, and restructuring, I excel at optimizing internal processes and guiding teams to achieve corporate goals. My multilingual skills and experience across diverse geographies enable me to deliver positive outcomes, even in complex, multicultural environments. I specialize in diagnosing issues, implementing solutions, and turning around what others deem unfixable."

Follow Fernanda Carvalho on Linkedin

https://www.linkedin.com/in/fernanda-carvalho

Website: https://www.fcconsultancy.biz/

The Power of Pacing Your Peaks

By Helen Farmer

I never thought I'd be the kind of person who would climb mountains in my forties, write a children's book, or start a radio career in my thirties, but here I am, doing all those things and more. Life has a funny way of surprising you, especially when you realize that the so-called "prime" of life is not behind you but very much in front of you – no matter what your age. I'm living proof that it's never too late to take on new challenges, discover hidden passions, or meet the people who will become your greatest supporters.

In my thirties, I found myself in a place of reinvention, starting a radio career at an age when many people are already established in their chosen fields. At the time, I didn't feel like I was late to the party. I felt like I was just getting started, dipping my toes into something new and exhilarating.

And that's one of the biggest lessons I've learned on this journey: it's okay to start late. In fact, I'd argue that starting later in life often comes with its own set of advantages – like life experience, resilience, and the ability to laugh at yourself when things don't go to plan.

But this isn't just about career changes. This is about the idea that your "peaks" in life – those moments of triumph, joy, and self-discovery – don't need to follow a prescribed timeline. We're often conditioned to believe that our twenties are for exploration, our thirties are for settling down, and by the time we hit our forties and beyond, we should have it all figured out. That's nonsense. Life doesn't happen in neat, linear stages. It's messy, unpredictable, and often full of wonderful surprises – if you let it be.

Take Kilimanjaro, for example. Climbing a mountain had always been on my list of things to do, but I hadn't gotten around to it. Like many of us, I was busy with the demands of work and family, juggling responsibilities and putting off the big dreams for "someday." Then age 40 was approaching, and something shifted. I 160ealized that someday needed to be now. So, I took the plunge and signed up to climb Mount Kilimanjaro. I trained hard, prepared myself mentally and physically, and then I did it. The experience was transformative – not just because of the physical accomplishment but because it taught me that it's never too late to challenge yourself. Or your perception of yourself.

I wish I could say that summiting Kilimanjaro was the peak of my story (pun intended!), but the truth is, there's always another mountain. The next time, I found myself on the glacial slopes of another summit, this time in Georgia. This year it was Uganda.

And what I learned from these experiences is that life, much like climbing a mountain, is all about pacing. You don't have to race to the top; you just have to keep putting one foot in front of the other, at your own pace, on your own terms.

Sometimes the climb feels endless, sometimes you want to give up, but there's always a view waiting for you – and often, the best views come when you've taken the time to enjoy the journey.

One of the greatest misconceptions we're fed is that success has a deadline. Whether it's in relationships, careers, or personal growth, we're told that if we don't achieve certain things by a certain age, we've missed the boat. I couldn't disagree more. I didn't meet my husband until my late twenties or start a family at what some might call the "ideal" age, but the timing was perfect for me. There's a wonderful freedom in letting go of the idea that life needs to happen on someone else's timeline. The truth is, you haven't even met all the people who will love you yet. That's such an exciting thought! Life will continue to surprise you with new friendships, relationships, and connections, no matter how old you are.

When I think about writing my children's book, I smile in

disbelief because it's something I never thought possible. It wasn't until I became a mum that the idea took root – and even then, I doubted myself. Who was I to write a children's book?

But what mattered was that I had a story and perspective to tell, a voice to share, and an audience of little ones (including my own kids!) who needed to hear it. So, I sat down and started writing. And once again, I learned that it's never too late to begin a new chapter – literally and figuratively.

The theme that ties all of these experiences together is simple: life is about pacing your peaks.

You don't have to reach the top in your twenties, thirties, or even forties. Your peaks can come at any time – as long as you keep climbing. Whether you're tackling a literal mountain, starting a new career, learning a new skill, or embarking on a new relationship, there's no expiration date on your potential.

The trick is to embrace the process, enjoy the view along the way, and trust that the best is always yet to come.

And while we're on the subject of timing, let me say this: you're never "too late" to find your tribe. I've met some of the most incredible people later in life – people who have become dear friends, mentors, and confidants. It's a comforting reminder that you haven't even met all of your people yet. There are still connections waiting to be made, relationships waiting to flourish, and communities waiting to embrace you. Whether it's through work, travel, or shared passions, life has a way of bringing the right people into your world when you're open to it.

So, if you're feeling stuck or wondering if you've missed your chance to chase a dream or make a change, I want to tell you this: you haven't. It's never too late to start again, to learn something new, or to pursue what lights you up inside.

The peaks you're meant to climb are out there, waiting for you – and the best part? You get to decide when and how you'll reach them.

Life isn't a race, and there's no deadline on your dreams. Take your time, pace yourself, and remember: the view from the top is worth every step.

About Helen Farmer

Helen Farmer is the author of My Mummy's Secret Adventures, a children's book that aims to help working mothers with the question of 'Where does mummy go all day?" inspired by her two daughters (and their endless questions).

She is also a well-known broadcaster on Dubai Eye 103.8FM, where she keeps the city entertained and informed with discussions on everything from finance to food every weekday afternoon.

When she's not on the air or writing, Helen shares snippets of her life on social media, offering a peek into her world, with a relatable mix of Dubai life, travel, style, and those real life parenting moments.

Follow Helen Farmer on Instagram @_helenfarmer_

Order "My Mummy's Secret Adventures here amzn.eu/d/ffC8Gim

REBEL CASESTUDIES

I'm always humbled when someone trusts me to help them, over the past years until now, (and future!). I feel so lucky to have such diversity of clients. One thing maybe they don't realize, is how much being part of their journeys and growth inspires me also. I wanted to share some of their stories to inspire you also. I curated 3 case studies for you!

LETTING GO OF THE 'PERFECT POST
BY
VINITA MICHAEL

NEVER LOOSING SIGHT OF WHY YOU
STARTED
BY VAYANA SALIM

HOW A PASTIME HOBBY DURING RAMADAN
TURNED INTO A MINI BIZ
BY AMMAL FARAHAT

LETTING GO OF THE 'PERFECT POST"
BY VINITA MICHAEL

Vinita Michael is *an award-winning jewelry designer and gemologist, Vinita Michael's eponymous jewelry label is a testament to the fusion of unique design and intricate craftsmanship. Specializing in exquisite jewelry and precious lifestyle products, Vinita has captivated the market with her visionary collections.*

I've had the privilege of working closely with Alex for nearly five years now, and the journey has been nothing short of transformative. Alex's insights into performance marketing and digital growth strategies have not only expanded my brand's reach. Her ability to adapt our strategy as my brand has evolved has been key in driving measurable growth.

Throughout my career, I've worn many hats—from designer to educator—and having Alex by my side has been invaluable. In addition to running my own brand, I've taken on the role of design educator with a renowned international body, expanding my contribution within the jewelry industry. No matter the phase of my journey, Alex has always been there as a trusted mentor, helping me navigate the complexities of the digital space and making sure I stay ahead of the curve."

I have done Fb ad + Insta ad course with Alex. Prior to taking the course, I was completely dependent on my marketing agencies ... spending considerable amounts repeatedly without any real returns ... I took Alex's course to become more knowledgeable to be honest ... But I was so ecstatic when I ran my first Fb ad myself for AED 200.00 and it generated AED 2000 in revenue within 24 hrs.!! This, by following Alex's pro tips! I remember frantically sending screenshots to Alex on DM! " It's working Alex! It's working! " lol ...Of course it had to, when you have Alex as your coach

"Done is better than perfected" – Alex

At times I can be overtly critical … and this need to have 'the perfect post / perfect reel was really slowing my progress' My favorite learning from Alex is: **"Done is better than perfected"** …

Now I'm not afraid to put things out there for feedback and constructive criticism. We are all learning and getting better every day..

What sets Alex apart is her entrepreneurial spirit. Like me, she built her business from the ground up, and that shared experience creates a deep understanding. Her creative, go-getter attitude and wealth of knowledge inspire me to continually push boundaries and elevate my business to new heights.

Follow on Instagram: @vinitamichaeljewelcraft
www.vinitamichael.com

HOW A PASTIME HOBBY DURING RAMADAN TURNED INTO A MINI BIZ
BY AMMAL FARAHAT

Ammal Farahat works with people who are seeking to balance professional and personal aspirations thus reducing stress & increasing satisfaction.

When I was introduced to Alex, I was trying to rediscover myself and if there is anything I could do as a career away from the corporate world, which I had been in for 20 years. I was 45 years old, looking to be an entrepreneur though I was told I am not entrepreneur material (are they right?), my weakness marketing and negotiations in a world of social media (everyone is so young, am I too old?). I knew I no longer wanted to do what I had been doing for the past 20 years, Quality Management & Customer Experience but what can I do? What do I have to offer? Why would anyone be interested?

"I WAS TOLD I AM NOT ENTREPRENEURIAL MATERIAL"

I felt I was too old to be on social media and if I am on a platform, I should act my age but I don't feel comfortable being someone I am not. Sometimes I am the calm wise person in the group but I am also the crazy one. Engrained in me, is the thought of what professional looks like and my colorful quirky side needs to be hidden if I want people to take me seriously, especially at my age. One of my biggest pain or challenges is money, professional means appearing to have lots of it and not caring about it. Talking about finances or payment or even putting a price for my fees was so painful I would offer services for free and then get angry with myself.

I started out slow, observing Alex on IG, checking out some of the accounts she talked about, watched her YouTube videos, taking notes and experimenting with what she says. If I had an opinion, thought or question I would post about it and interact with others on social media. While learning about branding from Alex, I got the chance to identify and explore all my skills and knowledge. With her encouragement I tested several areas and was able to get clients. Through these experiments I gained direction, clarity and inner peace. Then one day, I saw what Alex was always talking about "It's there, what you are good at and others need". An annual activity I was doing with my kids for the past 9 years. As soon as I "saw" it, developed and packaged it for others to use and apply. I sold out within 3 days at the price I felt was fair for my clients and myself. I even received overseas orders for next year.

"LEAN IN TO THE THINGS YOU LOVE! THE ANSWER'S ARE THERE!" - ALEX

Alex has a passion and energy about what she does and sharing it with others that is enormous. Sometimes it's hard to keep up but that's were good notes come in and that she records almost everything. I would go back reading through my notes as if I had a manual. Then I realized, the beauty of Alex is she encourages me to just go out there and do it, experiment, adjust and keep doing it. Trying to follow a "this is how it is", is good at times, but also restricts creativity. Alex encourages for self-expression and creativity "you do you" and this comes from her understanding and empathy for others mental wellbeing. In a world we're it's all about do, do, do, she does give reminders, it's OK to take a break and look after yourself. She is very comfortable with emotions and tears.

3 YEARS LATER... A NEW PATH FOR ZUMRATI!

Three years later, while pondering how to propel Zumrati forward, a significant family event – my youngest sister's impending wedding – demanded my attention. Recognizing the need to prioritize, I made the difficult choice to step back temporarily from the business realm.

This hiatus aimed to focus on the wedding and reevaluate my commitment to Zumrati. Struggling to envision its growth, I decided to reassess my path, realizing my fixation on trifle matters hindered my grasp of the broader picture. Amid wedding preparations, an unexpected opportunity arose: a tour guiding certification program. Leveraging my multilingual skills and expertise as a stress coach, I ventured into freelance tour guiding.

Navigating branding, marketing, and negotiating contracts by applying the knowledge and skills I gained from Alex for Zumrati. This was effortless and stress free thus the new question became: Did this divergence signify a transition from Zumrati to a career in tourism?

The question was a painful one which I struggled with. However, once I let go of the internal struggle embracing curiosity, possibilities emerged. Engaging with diverse individuals as a tour guide unveiled fresh marketing avenues, fostering collaborations with businesses and inquiries for family coaching services. The narrative of Zumrati, once a mystery, began to unravel gradually, revealing new horizons and prospects. Zumrati still had a place in my life, just in a different capacity than I'd originally envisioned. It gave me a chance to connect with people on a deeper level, sharing not only the beauty of my homeland but also the values and practices that Zumrati stand for. One memorable experience was guiding a lady who had suffered a recent illness and loss. She had given up on building any connections with friends and family. Through our conversations, we realized my skills as a stress coach and my experiences with Zumrati provided her with more than just a tour, she gained emotional support and tools to rebuild her sense of unity with her family.

This experience reinforced the idea that Zumrati and my new path were not mutually exclusive but rather complementary. I found a rhythm that allowed me to nurture both my roles.

I am working on hosting specialized tours that included elements of family bonding and stress management. This unique offering sets me apart in the tourism industry and brings me a renewed sense of purpose to my work.

Zumrati isn't just a business or a brand; it is an extension of my life's mission to foster connection, resilience, and joy among families. As I look ahead, I am excited about the endless possibilities that lie before me.

Follow Ammal Farahat on IG @livingquality & @zumrati_ksa

SELLING MORE ONLINE ON A WEEKEND THEN EVER BEFORE & NEVER LOOSING SIGHT OF WHY YOU STARTED
BY VAYANA SALIM

Vayana is the founder & creator behind the kid's clothes business Vay's Kingdom. Her very own sewing business, hand-making baby and toddler colorful products using only organic material (certified Oeko-tex or GOTS fabrics)

I needed someone to help me structure my work. Someone who could show me how to do things like social media, create a launch campaign, put stories together, activate my social media in a way. Also needed help with setting my website automation. I basically needed help to structure my work and showing me, practically taking my hand and doing it with me, so I could reach the objectives I had. I struggled to structure my work, with overthinking everything that I was doing, not confident with my work (thinking it was not good), overwhelmed with the amount of task I was pressuring myself to do.

Working with Alex helped on a lot of aspects. It helps me stay focus, after each session, I know what I have to do next, I know I'm not alone in this, she's always here to support if needed. We set a clear action plan on what needs to be done during the coming days. I started working with her to get help on launching a limited edition. A plan was put together, stories created, post, newsletter, the plan was actionable for me and realistic to follow. When the collection was launched, I sold more online in a weekend that I did with any other collection before.

"Don't listen to people around you unless they want to lift you up!"

Working with Alex is a blessing in the sky. She knows her sh.., and she quickly understood what type of small business owner I was and what kind of help I needed from her. I also knew where I needed help from but she didn't try to help on part where I didn't need to. She is fast, so you have to keep up! She is easy to talk to and I've never felt judge or shy of saying something silly in front of her. All guards down the moment I sit and work with her. I genuinely feel that with her, nothing is impossible, I can achieve anything, plus the amount of energy she brings to the room is amazing and contagious.

I feel you; it isn't easy. The road is full of ups and downs but do not lose sight of why you started, don't listen to people around you unless they want to lift you up!

Everybody else doesn't matter, it is your journey and only you know what is good for you. Make sure you enjoy all the steps along the way, what you're doing is pretty amazing and not many people have the balls to do it, don't forget that.

I wish I understood earlier that I couldn't do it all by myself. That asking for help or support didn't mean I was unable to do it, in the contrary, it means I know how to get my ship move in the best way possible.

**Follow Vay's Kingdom on Instagram @vayskingdom
www.vayskingdom.com**

BONUS CONTENT

20 Steps to Turn Your Passion into Profitable Mini Empire

STEP 1

WHAT ARE YOU GOOD AT? Aka YOUR SUPA POWERS!

PLAY TO YOUR STRENGTHS -

Often, people look at what others are doing, search for quick ways to make money, or follow the latest trending hack. Let me be straight with you: most of the time, these quick fixes, if they even work, only give you short-term rewards. Now, if you're serious about making money, doing stuff you love, and... ready for it: being able to sustain doing it for the long haul, even when times get tough, and still actually enjoy it (wait, Alex... you mean even when it gets hard, I'll enjoy it?), then hear me out on this first step. This sets the foundation for any success you're aiming to achieve.

When you create a business or side hustle out of something you genuinely LOVE... boom... you've unlocked it all. When we love something, we get attached to it, we want to spend time doing it, and most importantly: IT MAKES US DAMN HAPPY! We shine, we smile, we are more energetic and optimistic. Spend a long time at a job you hate, and even the happiest human will get depressed. (That was me!)

So, bottom line for STEP 1: Play to your strengths, the answer might be right in front of you! (Read the case study story XX) Pay massive attention to the things you spend your spare time doing, reading, talking about, hobbies, etc..... It's right there!

HOMEWORK EXERCISE:
Make a list. Think about what you already do in your spare time, hobbies, what you love and enjoy! Hey! You can even ask close friends what they think you are good at!

STEP 2

WHAT PROBLEMS DO YOUR SUPER POWERS SOLVE?

YOUR SKILLS OR WHAT YOU ARE DOING - WHAT PROBLEMS IS IT SOLVING?

This is an important step to flesh out and is often super overlooked! How will this benefit you?

- **Brainstorming:** This will help you unlock all the ways you can create products and services, and in return, help you see how many revenue streams your idea can generate.
- Once you identify the problems, you'll get a clear picture of who your target audience is.
- If you are clear about what problems you solve, you will have clarity on HOW you will fix them. You'll be able to come up with many ways to deliver your solutions.
- This step will help you gather the messaging copy you need for your website, social media content, and promo videos.

HOMEWORK EXERCISE:
Write down all the ways your skills or talents can help people.

IT'S A GOOD DAY TO BE A REBEL

STEP 3

WHO IS YOUR MVP?

TO NICHE OR NOT TO NICHE

It is important to know who you want to focus on. Coming off Step 2, you'll now have a better understanding of who is experiencing the problems you can solve with your superpowers! Defining this is crucial as it will help later with your messaging, copywriting, targeting, and many other marketing, branding, and sales tactics.

Now, I'm going to make things a little challenging. Just bear with me… Sometimes, we may not be too sure, or the spectrum is quite broad. This is not a problem but an opportunity! In simple terms, you'll put out all your 'honey,' and you'll let the bees come to you!

For example, I could have really niched down to "only work with SMBs," but I didn't, even to this day. Yes, I do have key demographics; I focus on entrepreneurs, SMBs, freelancers, and marketers, but because I didn't develop a positioning that would limit me too much, now, five years in, I even teach kids! Wow, yes!

Bottom line: be careful not to niche down too much, as it might limit opportunities. But, depending on what you'll be doing, at times it's good to stay specific. Use your common sense based on what I've guided you with.

HOMEWORK EXERCISE:
Make a list of who you think could be your potential ideal target audience.

IT'S A GOOD DAY TO BE A REBEL

STEP 4

STRUCTURE YOUR OFFERING

CONVERSIONS GALORE

Sounds obvious, right? Well, it's not. While writing this chapter, I had a client session where she told me she wasn't getting many clients. Then I found out she had no structure to her services.

One of the key factors that influence people to work with you is having clarity in how that is done. Just like with e-commerce, or when ordering takeout, we like a straightforward experience and clarity on what our options are. It's the same with your offerings.

So, make sure you are placing structure into this. It can be anything you see fit, from package hours, daily rates, hourly rates, bundle prices, or custom rates based on scope—even "let's grab a coffee, and I'll tell you!" Hahaha, for real! Place this on your site, portfolio, WhatsApp for business, email, your forehead, but have it!

HOMEWORK EXERCISE:
Flesh out your structure. Don't overcomplicate it. Less is more to start with, and as time goes on, you'll see what works.

STEP 5

PRICING YOUR OFFERING

NO MONEY, NO HONEY!

I know, I know—so many of you struggle with this part because, as I hear you saying, talking about money makes you feel "yucky." Well, wake up. To make this a business, you need pricing, and you need to be confident about it. Just remove the emotion from it and look at it from a practical standpoint. Many entrepreneurs fail because they are too emotionally attached to certain aspects of the business. Use emotion to fuel your motivation, but keep it out of key decisions that will help your business grow.

Ways to help you figure out your cost:

- Look at the market average in your niche so you are not too low or too high to start with.
- You can always start at a lower price and work your way up as demand increases.
- Rates evolve. They don't have to be set in stone forever; this is just to get you started.

HOMEWORK EXERCISE:
Make a decision on your pricing and stick to it for a while.

IT'S A GOOD DAY TO BE A REBEL

STEP 6

DEFINE YOUR BRAND

What is branding, you may be asking? Here's a quick exercise: Think about one of your favorite brands! Go… quick! Now that you have a name, say out loud or write down three adjectives that you associate with your favorite brand. Got it? Now, I bet that if not all three, at least two of them are adjectives connected to emotion. Am I right?

Branding is about the emotion you create, the aspirational feeling. What emotion are you really selling? For me, it's energy!

HOMEWORK EXERCISE:

- What are your three brand values?
- Does your brand have a mission? (practical aspect)
- What are five personality traits that describe your brand?

ASK YOURSELF:

- "WHAT DO I WANT PEOPLE TO FEEL WHEN THEY INTERACT WITH MY BRAND?"
- "WHAT FIRST IMPRESSION DO I WANT TO CREATE?"
- "AND WHAT FEELING DO I WANT TO LEAVE PEOPLE WITH?"

STEP 7

BUILD A SALES PAGE / MINI SITE

No matter the size of your hustle, a sales page or mini-site can make a huge difference in how you grow, scale, and create a lasting first impression! People aren't hanging out on websites the way they are on TikTok, LinkedIn, or Instagram, but here's a quick-fire look at how a mini-site or sales page can fire up your business right away!

- You need to have free content that is longer-lasting and more impactful to give away (more on this next!). These will need to be hosted on your site and will be email-gated! Not only are you providing value, but you will also be able to nurture these contacts with email series, even WhatsApp messages!
- When interested people come to your site for your freemiums (you need to be creating awareness for these), they will be exposed to all the other great things you offer!
- When you meet people, you can share your business card with your info and let them know they can find everything there!
- If someone inquires about your services, you'll look super professional by pointing them to your site.
- If people search online for your services, you can be discoverable on Google, which is highly beneficial!

What is the difference between a sales page & a mini-site, you may be thinking?

Ok, let's simplify. A SALES PAGE IS:

- Focused on a specific product/service you are selling.
- There is no other information besides what you are selling and seeking a lead or conversion.
- On your website, you can have pages that are sales pages (you can check some of mine!) because they are specific to

selling services! You will also have other pages that are, as I call them, "soft sales pages," more about educating and providing information.

ULTIMATELY: A sales page consists of structured content designed to drive leads and conversions.
**Purpose of a sales

STEP 8

NURTURING YOUR SALES FUNNEL LEADS

Your Freemium builds the middle layer of your Sales Funnel. It will give you emails; you'll work with a CRM like Mailchimp or Klavio, allowing you to create an email series to bring your people value weekly. Bottom line, here you will have captured people's data so you can send email newsletters, make calls, write custom emails, and send messages to these groups of people.

HOMEWORK EXERCISE:
Think about how and what is the best way to keep nourishing your leads.

IT'S A GOOD DAY TO BE A REBEL

STEP 9

CREATE, CREATE CONTENT

HOW MUCH DO YOU REALLY CARE?

Truth is, if you don't care about creating a community that you want to deliver value to, whether it be through entertaining, funny videos, music, art, educational content—how can you expect people to care for you and do business with you?

Content can be: EDUCATIONAL, INSPIRATIONAL, ENTERTAINMENT, EDUTAINMENT
PLATFORMS WITH THE BIGGEST OPPORTUNITY RIGHT NOW:

- TIK TOK
- LINKEDIN
- INSTAGRAM

HOMEWORK EXERCISE:
Create content pillars around topics that you can consistently create content for over a long period. Content needs to be daily!

IT'S A GOOD DAY TO BE A REBEL

STEP 10

GIVING FREE VALUABLE CONTENT THAT IS LONGER-LASTING AND HAS MORE DEPTH – FREEMIUMS

Apart from your daily content on social media, by creating freemiums, you'll be able to level up your impact on the people you want to reach. FREEMIUMS are pieces of content or experiences that people can access from you by providing some of their data (emails, contacts), granting them access to something that will serve as EDUCATIONAL, INSPIRATIONAL, ENTERTAINMENT, or EDUTAINMENT content. This could be a free 101 session with you, a small amount of work you do for free, an e-book guide, downloadable content, VIP video access... the ideas are endless.

- For people to gain access, make sure they provide their details (email, name, phone number). Only then can they access your freemium.
- Place this on your sales page.

HOMEWORK EXERCISE:
Ask yourself, what would serve your desired people the most value? Then do it!
Remember to refresh these from time to time. Ensure they bring value and do not make people feel trapped in a hard-core sales funnel. Those are terrible!

WHEN YOU GIVE, GIVE! WHEN YOU ASK, ASK! BE CLEAR. DON'T MAKE YOUR POTENTIAL CUSTOMERS FEEL TRAPPED!

STEP 11

COMMUNITY IS POWER!

There is a difference between having many followers on your socials versus having a community. Oh yes, community means you actually have people who care about you! To achieve this takes creating content that matters, being multi-dimensional with your content, showing up consistently, and always striving to understand how to deliver value to your audience.

What is Multi-dimensional content? Content that goes beyond your area of expertise: your hobbies, passions, opinions, points of view, travels, etc.

Action Items + Ideas:

- Pay attention to what content performs best and double down on it.
- Do Q&A sessions, answer questions.
- Engage in comments & DMs.
- Surprise & delight + giveaways.
- Do LIVE content.
- Spend 1 hour daily networking in the comments on social pages, delivering value.

STEP 12

COLLABORATIONS & PARTNERSHIPS

If you've read my book, you'll have learned about my case study with Crimson Hexagon. The right collaborations can uplift your brand, giving you access to a new audience.

HOMEWORK EXERCISE:
What brands, creators, experts, thought leaders, and influencers will bring value and make sense for you to collaborate with? Explore using hashtags to find them. Make sure to check their profiles and community engagement.

STEP 13

HOW TO ACTUALLY SELL!

My best advice, based on how it's worked massively well for me, is to be very transparent when selling. Ok, what do I mean by this?! Especially if you are leveraging your personal brand and you have books, courses, programs, etc.

When you want to sell, sell confidently. When you're giving free value, do it with generosity. What I don't want you to do is those hard-core funnels and traps that only make people feel deceived. For example, don't offer a "free" class that only upsells to a paid service. Don't just show up when you want to sell something. Don't be stingy, offering one tiny taste and then funneling me to buy the rest.

If you wouldn't like this feeling yourself, don't do it to your people and potential new clients. Here's a great example of being transparent: Imagine hosting a free live class or an in-person class where you deliver a great experience. At the end, you can absolutely say, "If you want to hire/book/buy my XYZ, talk to me or head to my site!" No one felt trapped or deceived; they got their free value, and you were direct about what you're selling! Boom! People are not fools; they will appreciate your honesty. I've always done this, and it works so well.

HOMEWORK EXERCISE:
Revise how you have been approaching your sales strategy.

IT'S A GOOD DAY TO BE A REBEL

STEP 14

FIRE UP YOUR MARKETING

Think of marketing like sprinkles on a cupcake, the nut to the tella, hahaha! It's really the spark that your business needs, and as many of my clients say, "Oh wow, this stuff really works!" Become good at practicing tactics and strategies so you see what works with your audience! Inside my Free Rebel Academy, you will find many courses on this.

HOMEWORK EXERCISE:
Consider if you want to do a campaign, product launch, flash sale, special value offer, or seasonal promotions. There are so many options. Look at my free courses!

- Think about your marketing plans for every month, or as often as you can.
- Marketing ideas based on holidays, special days, and seasons work really well.
- Plan your marketing strategies based on your sales funnel:
  - Cold > What tactics/strategies attract new leads?
  - Warm > For people who are already familiar with you, what can you do to push for conversions?
  - Hot > Start here! It's much easier to upsell to those who have already bought from you!
  - Watch my sales funnel masterclass on this.

STEP 15

HOW MUCH IT'S COSTING YOU TO RUN THIS MINI-BIZ OR SIDE HUSTLE?

This is crucial; I can't emphasize enough how important it is for you to have your business finances and costs organized and managed. If you're not good at this, hire a finance manager or coach to help you. Your business will grow if your costs and finances are well managed.

Common Mistakes:

- Mixing personal money with business money.
- Having no clarity on business costs.
- Not knowing where you stand financially each month.
- Not revising your lifestyle plan to lower costs.

HOMEWORK EXERCISE:
Work out how much it costs to run your side hustle. Consider every single detail.

STEP 16

WORK TOWARDS BREAKING EVEN

You need to be making money. Money is the oxygen for your business, and only when you're building revenue and making profit can you truly start to have a business. Aim to reach a break-even point.

Caveat: If you're leveraging your personal brand, it may take time. As I've explained before, you need to create content, build community, develop your brand, earn trust, and understand that monetization can take time. If you really need money to cover essentials like rent or food, consider getting a part-time job to provide the cash flow you need, giving your business the bandwidth it needs to succeed.

IT'S A GOOD DAY TO BE A REBEL

STEP 17

REVENUE STREAMS

How many ways can you sell what you do? This is essentially what you want to ask yourself to unlock a ton of ideas. There are so many models out there. But as you start to make money, you'll want to scale and grow by having more than one revenue stream. I started my first year with two, moved to three, and quickly to four. I also experimented a lot and still do—I love it as it helps me understand what people want and need.

HOMEWORK EXERCISE:
How many ways can you sell what you do?

STEP 18

INVEST BACK IN THE AREAS THAT WILL HELP YOU GROW

If you are serious about wanting to grow and scale, you need to keep reinvesting the money your business makes back into it, especially in areas that will help you grow. This could be your social content, hiring staff, or consulting support.

HOMEWORK EXERCISE:
How many ways can you sell what you do? What areas need investment to grow? What areas do you need support in?

STEP 19

LEARN TO LOVE TO PIVOT!

To stay alive, you need to innovate.

One of the key traits of a successful entrepreneur is the ability to change, pivot, adapt, and be agile. Consumer behavior changes, the world shifts—look at what happened with COVID. Pay close attention to consumer behavior, culture, and your customers' needs and aspirations. Think outside the box & listen to the market! Come up with new ideas and try new models. Don't be afraid to experiment. You won't always get it perfect, but by constantly trying and testing, you'll find winning ideas!

HOMEWORK EXERCISE:
When was the last time you came up with a new way of doing things? Do you deal well with change? Do you resist it? Are you an overthinker?

STEP 20

ARE YOU FREAKING ENJOYING THE JOURNEY?

The most important part of it all! All that matters is, are you enjoying the process? Is the journey fulfilling you? Because if not, you won't be able to sustain it for however long you want to keep at it. The process is everything. Love the ride you are on. Be present, focused, and aligned with what matters most to you.

HOMEWORK EXERCISE:
Is the journey, the process making you happy?

QUICK FIRE PLAN

1. **DECONSTRUCT A BIG IDEA INTO SMALL BUILDING BLOCKS THAT ARE REALISTIC TO:**
   - Your ambitions
   - Time you have
   - Money/Budget to invest
   - Skills/Your talents
   - How much experience you have or want to gain?
   - Resources you need
   - Lifestyle
   - Country/City you are in
   - Stuff you absolutely know you need help with or can't do

Action Point:

Write down in detail the answer to each point as much as you can.

Don't be hard on yourself. Don't be emotional—be practical.
YES, HAVE PASSION. USE IT AS FUEL TO NEVER GIVE UP!

ABOUT THE AUTHOR

ALEXANDRA CARVALHO

I HELP ENTREPRENEURS & PERSONAL BRANDS GROW AND ADAPT IN THE EVER-CHANGING WORLD OF SOCIAL MEDIA MARKETING BY GIVING YOU BUSINESS & CREATIVE STRATEGIES THAT FIT YOUR GOALS & AMBITION LEVELS

Alex is the founder and creative strategist of Alex's House of Social. With over 17+ years of digital marketing prowess, she's conquered both agency realms and ventured into the entrepreneurial landscape, launching House of Social, her self-funded venture for the past 8 years. Results? Multiple 6 to 7 figures and counting. Her published book " It's a Good Day To Be A Rebel" made it to 4th on Amazon's social media best-seller list.

Over 5,000 people have attended her sell-out boot camps, masterclasses, and short courses. The free online Rebel Academy streams over 50+ free courses and hosts 5k I students. Her client base expands through the UAE, Europe, United States and all over the world. She's not just a consultant; she's a marketing and educational powerhouse, and a keynote speaker.Her mission is empowering individuals to make a bold statement with their marketing, fostering growth not only for their businesses but for their personal brands. Alex's strong creative pulse on the current media landscape and big energy make her one of the most passionate hybrid social minds of her generation.

She's been featured on Forbes, Entrepreneur Middle East, Campaign Middle East and is a frequent guest on the Dubai Eye

Radio. She's also been a creative juror for the Cannes Lions Roger Hatchuel Student Academy.

FOLLOW ALEX ON
INSTAGRAM @ALEXHOUSEOFSOCIAL
TIK TOK @ALEXHOUSEOFSOCIAL
YOU TUBE @ALEXHOUSEOFSOCIAL
SNAPCHAT @ALEXHOUSEOFSOCIAL

FOR EVERYTHING ALEX'S HOUSE OF SOCIAL
FREE REBEL ACADEMY
REBEL CLUB
REBEL SHOP
YACHTCLASS
GO TO WWW.ALEXHOUSEOFSOCIAL.COM

REBEL NOTES

YOU'RE UNSTOPPABLE

CHOOSE TO BELIEVE THAT

YOU CAN AND YOU WILL

STOP GIVING A S****** ABOUT WHAT OTHERS THINK OF YOU!

BE WEIRD SO OTHER

WEIRDOS

CAN FIND YOU

YOU ONLY NEED TO MAKE SENSE

FOR YOURSELF NOT OTHERS

UNTIL YOU DON'T DO IT YOU WILL NEVER KNOW

YOU GOT THIS

Printed in Great Britain
by Amazon

5c14077f-f9eb-4b9c-82be-ed5a3673aaf0R01